LETTER WRITING *Made Easy*

LETTER WRITING *Made Easy*

THE RIGHT COMMUNICATION FOR THE RIGHT OCCASION

MARGARET McCARTHY

JAICO PUBLISHING HOUSE

Ahmedabad Bangalore Chennai
Delhi Hyderabad Kolkata Mumbai

Published by Jaico Publishing House
A-2 Jash Chambers, 7-A Sir Phirozshah Mehta Road
Fort, Mumbai - 400 001
jaicopub@jaicobooks.com
www.jaicobooks.com

Published in arrangement with:
Santa Monica Press, LLC
215 South Highway 101, Suite 110
Solana Beach, CA 92075, USA

To be sold only in India, Bangladesh, Bhutan,
Pakistan, Nepal, Sri Lanka and the Maldives.

LETTER WRITING MADE EASY
ISBN 978-81-8495-995-6

First Jaico Impression: 2017

Printed by
Trinity Academy For Corporate Training Limited, Mumbai

Contents

Business Letters 75

Introduction

People often wonder in this modern age why letters are even necessary anymore. Isn't it easier and quicker to just pick up the phone? Sure it is. But is it as effective as a letter?

Never underestimate the power of the written word. The fact is, there are many occasions and situations in which personal letters make a great impact. And since more people today would rather just use the phone, the fact that you have taken the time to choose your words carefully and write a letter carries even more weight—the recipient will be doubly impressed, and your message will hit home.

Part of the reluctance of most people to write a letter is a simple lack of knowledge. Frankly, it seems that only a small percentage of our society—mostly secretaries—understands how to format a formal business letter.

What constitutes a good letter? How should it be laid out? Do you have to type it? Are there any special tricks that you must know?

In this book, I will answer these questions and more. I will show you how to write intimate personal letters and powerful business correspondence. I will also offer practical advice on format, style, tone, forms of address, etc.

Best of all, I have provided ready-to-use samples for hundreds of common occasions. All you need to do is plug in the details. In some cases, you'll want to vary certain particulars to fit your circumstances—*Letter Writing Made Easy!* is in no way a substitute for common sense. It merely hopes to help you write the best letter you can, and in turn, help you get the most out of situations in life that demand effective communication.

Personal Letters

Despite the fact that modern technology has made typing letters easier via word processors and computers—not to mention the fact that these letters can now be faxed or even electronically mailed—there is still nothing more effective than a *handwritten* personal letter.

Using your own hand conveys intimacy, informality, and a sense of your own style. It leaves no doubt that it was you who wrote it.

Because personal letters contain messages of the utmost importance—after all, there is nothing more important in life than friends and family—they must be worded carefully in order to avoid any possibility of misinterpretation.

With that in mind, here are a few guidelines to writing intimate personal letters.

- Write the date at the top of the first page, but do not include your return address or the recipient's address. It is considerate to date a letter to let the recipient know when it was written, but adding the formality of addresses is inappropriate for a personal touch.

- Always greet the recipient using his or her first name. If this seems too informal in a particular circumstance, then you are probably writing a business letter, and should format it as such (see the introduction for business letters).

- After the recipient's first name, use a comma. This is one key distinction between personal and business letters (which use colons). For example, if you are writing to your child's schoolteacher, and your only relationship to her is as her student's parent, then a formal business format is called for, i.e., **"Dear Mrs. Olson:"**. On the other hand, if she just happens to be an old, dear friend with whom you are on a first-name basis, then your letter will be handwritten and addressed, **"Dear Mary,"**.

• After the salutation, indent the first line of each paragraph.

• Sign off your letter with a close that reflects the nature of your relationship to the recipient, such as "Fondly," "Affectionately," "Love," or "Best regards."

• Use these sample letters as guidelines only. You will notice that most of them get right to the point, avoiding the "small talk" you find in most personal letters. That is because the small talk is up to you. So if you feel more comfortable opening your letter with a few "how are yous" and updates on your personal life, by all means do so. Again, if you team your own common sense with the information here, you'll be writing intimate personal letters in no time!

ONE

Apologies

We all make mistakes. Some are more serious than others, and sometimes it takes friends and loved ones a long time to forgive and forget.

In these cases, a sensitively written letter is a godsend. It allows you the freedom to gather your thoughts and select your words carefully. Additionally, if the recipient is not ready to speak to you personally, you can convey your message to them without that immediate contact.

In situations in which a long time has passed, a letter is even more appropriate. If you had a falling-out with a loved one, you don't want to just call him or her out of the blue one day. It is far more appropriate—and respectful—to send a letter. You can choose to break the ice or just open the door a little towards further communication.

One caveat: Never hedge on your apology. Do not say "I am sorry, but I believe I was right..." This instantly negates the apology, and defeats your purpose. If you cannot bring yourself to offer an unqualified apology, then the time is not right for a reconciliation.

In most cases, a well-written letter will open up communication. But if it doesn't, don't beat a dead horse. Just be patient and try again later.

Belated Thank-You for Gift

Dear (**name**),

Please forgive me for not writing to you sooner to thank you for the lovely (**type of gift**). Life has been extremely hectic as of late, and I feel awful about not having expressed my gratitude.

It was extremely thoughtful and generous of you to buy the (**type of gift**) for me, and I have been enjoying it very much. Every time I (**see/use**) it, I will think of you!

Love,

Belated Thank-You for Service or Favor

Dear (**name**),

Please forgive me for not writing to you sooner in appreciation of (**service or favor provided**). I can't thank you enough, and I would not want you to interpret my tardiness in writing to you as a reflection of a lack of gratitude on my part. (**Service or favor provided**) was of great help to me.

Please do not hesitate to call or write if I can be of some assistance to you.

Warmly,

Clearing the Air

Dear (**name**),

Well, after all this time I found myself thinking about you today. I realized what a shame it was that we haven't spoken in so long, and I'd like to make amends and resume our great friendship.

For my part, I'm sorry about (**describe nature of dispute**). Although neither one of us is likely to change that much, I do think we can resolve this problem and move on, so we can enjoy more great times ahead. We've been friends too long to let such a little matter destroy our relationship.

I miss you greatly. What do you say we get together for (**lunch/dinner**) next week, my treat? We can catch up on all we've been missing. I'll call you soon.

Friends again,

Forgot Anniversary of Employment

Dear (**name**),

Please forgive my embarrassing oversight of having forgotten the anniversary of your employment. It certainly was not intentional, and I hope I can make it up to you.

In fact, it is even more dismaying when I consider the high quality of your work and dedication to your job. I couldn't be more pleased with your performance.

So please accept my belated congratulations on the occasion. I sincerely hope you'll be on board for a long time to come.

Best regards,

I'm Sorry I didn't Return Your...

Dear **(name)**,

Please forgive me for not returning your **(name of item)** sooner. It was extremely helpful and I can't thank you enough. You were very kind to have lent me this **(name of item)**. I hope you haven't been inconvenienced by my tardiness in getting it back to you. If there is anything I can do for you, please do not hesitate to ask.

Sincerely,

I'm Sorry I Forgot Your Birthday

Dear **(name)**,

I'm so sorry I forgot your birthday! Can you ever forgive me? Please let me make it up to you.

How about if I take you to lunch? Are you free on **(day)**? I know of a wonderful **(type of food)** restaurant that I think you'll enjoy. I'll call you on **(day)** to set up a time when we can get together. I look forward to seeing you and do hope you will forgive my embarrassing oversight.

Best wishes,

Inappropriate Remark

Dear (**name**),

I deeply regret the unfortunate outburst I made on (**day**), and I hope you'll accept my apology.

I am sometimes prone to speak impulsively, and it is a habit I am trying hard to change. I hope you'll allow me to make up for the embarrassment I caused you at your (**event/party**).

Thank you for understanding.

Best regards,

Payment is Late

Dear (**name**),

You were so kind to loan me this money that I feel just awful that I am late in repaying you. Finances have been tight lately, but I have managed to come up with (**some of what/the full amount that**) I owe you, which I have enclosed.

I hope that this will suffice, and that our friendship has not been unduly affected by my irresponsibility. How about if I treat you to lunch next week? I'll call you soon to arrange the details.

Sincerely,

Taking Responsibility for Property Damage

Dear (**name**),

I feel just terrible about the unfortunate damage (**I/my son/daughter/etc.**) caused to (**your item**). I intend to take full responsibility for (**replacing/repairing**) it.

It was very kind of you to dismiss the damage as merely accidental, but I just won't feel right until your item is restored to its original condition.

I hope you don't mind that I contacted a (**repair/replacement**) company to arrange for an estimate, and I would appreciate it if you would let me know the best time for them to drop by without inconveniencing you any further.

Please accept my apologies, and I hope we can quickly put this unfortunate incident behind us and continue our wonderful friendship.

Best regards,

Unseemly Behavior of Guest

Dear (**name**),

Please accept my apologies for the unfortunate incident that occurred during our recent (**party/event**).

We believe the behavior was inappropriate, and we do not condone the remarks made by (**name of guest**). We regret any embarrassment or unpleasantness this may have caused you, and we wish to assure you that this sort of incident will never happen again.

Thank you for your understanding, and we look forward to sharing your company on a future occasion.

Sincerely,

TWO

Asking for a Favor

When you need a favor from a friend or relative, there is no better way to voice your request than in a letter. Its powers of persuasion are mighty!

Always be respectful and cordial, and indicate the purpose of your request clearly. If possible, try to convince the recipient why his or her favor will be valuable.

If you are unsure of your intentions, or your notion is vague, your chances of a favorable response are slim. But composing a letter will help you flesh out your thoughts on the matter, and thus ensure a request that is direct and thoroughly considered, so that a positive response is almost guaranteed!

Allowing a Friend or Relative to Spend the Night

Dear **(name)**,

My **(good friend/cousin/brother/etc.)**, **(name of guest)**, will be visiting **(name of town)** on **(date)**. Would it be possible for **(him/her)** to spend the night at your home? I wouldn't ask if it weren't for the fact that **(name of friend or relative)** and I are very close and I know what type of person **(he/she)** is. I also know that **(his/her)** finances are tight and that hotels are expensive in your area.

I really think that you and **(name of friend or relative)** would hit it off well. You have many of the same interests and are approximately the same age. Please give me a call as soon as possible to let me know if this would be all right with you.

Sincerely,

Job for Friend or Relative

Dear **(name)**,

I am sending you the resumé of **(my good friend/ cousin/brother/etc.)**, **(name of friend or relative)**, in the hope that you might find a place for **(him/her)** in your company. (**Name of friend or relative**) is an intelligent, honest, hard-working young (**man/woman**). I have known (**him/her**) for (**number of years**), and believe that (**he/she**) could become an extremely valuable employee for you and your company.

If there are no positions available at your company, do you know of any other openings where (**name of friend or relative's**) skills could be utilized? (**Name of friend or relative**) and I would appreciate any help you could lend on this matter.

Warmest regards,

Personal Recommendation

Dear (**name**),

I have known (**name of person being recommended**) for (**number**) years, and during that period of time I have found (**him/her**) to be a person of the highest caliber. Aside from being intelligent, honest, and hard-working, (**he/she**) is extremely easy to get along with. If you choose to employ (**name**), I am certain that you will find (**him/her**) a joy to work with.

I sincerely hope that you will decide to hire (**name**); (**he/she**) is someone I can recommend with complete and total confidence.

Cordially,

Recommending a Prospective Student

Dear (**name of admissions officer**),

I am writing to you in regard to a young (**friend/student/nephew/niece/etc.**) of mine, who has recently applied for admission to your fine institution. In the number of years I have known (**name**), (**he/she**) has always impressed me as a young person of exceptional quality. (**He/she**) is bright, dedicated, and studious, and I believe (**he/she**) would make an excellent addition to your freshman class next year.

I sincerely hope you will give serious consideration to (**name**). I would be happy to offer more specific details on this fine candidate should the need arise.

Best regards,

Requesting a Loan

Dear (**name**),

We've been friends for (**number**) years, and I wouldn't dream of imposing on you unless it was a matter of great importance; however, an unfortunate situation has arisen in our lives which we must try to overcome, and we're hoping you can help.

(Describe situation—husband/wife has lost job, skyrocketing medical bills, etc.), and we are finding ourselves rather lacking financially. It would be a godsend if you could loan us **(amount)**, which we will gladly repay you by **(date)**, or sooner if we're on our feet before then. Of course, I am only too happy to help you in any way that I can as well.

Thank you, **(name)**, for being such a great friend, and for being so attentive and helpful. You'll always have a special place in our hearts.

Best regards,

THREE

Condolence

In a time of tragedy, it is natural to respect the privacy of a loved one and simply step aside. The fact that it is extremely difficult to find the right words to convey sympathy and condolence only add to the challenge of doing—and saying—the right thing.

So a letter is the perfect solution. It is not imposing, and it allows you the time to choose your words carefully, which, under the circumstances, is optimal.

Brevity is highly recommended—again, a lengthy letter may seem too imposing in a time of grief. It is appropriate, however, to express support and share a fond memory. This will gently ease the recipient's burden and make he or she feel less alone. And when the grieving period is over, your gesture will long be remembered and appreciated.

Death of Child

Dear (**name**),

I cannot begin to express how profoundly saddened I am by the loss of (**name of child**). Please accept my deepest sympathy, and understand that I am always here to help if you need anything.

(**Name of child**) was a very special child, and I will always treasure the time I spent with (**him/her**) and remember (**him/her**) fondly, especially (**his/her**) generous spirit and love. I'm sure that wherever (**he/she**) is now, (**he/she**) is spreading the same joy. We're all blessed to have known (**him/her**).

I understand that you need time to be alone for awhile, but again, I wish to offer my help during this difficult period. Please do not hesitate to call if there is anything I can do.

Affectionately,

Death of Friend

Dear (**name**),

I was saddened to learn of the passing of your special friend, (**name**). Although I didn't know (**him/her**) as well as you did, I always admired (**him/her**) and will remember (**him/her**) fondly. Please convey my sympathy to (**his/her**) family.

I hope I can be of help during this difficult period, so if there is anything I can do, please don't hesitate to call me.

Affectionately,

Death of Husband or Wife

Dear (**name**),

Experiencing the death of a (**husband/wife**) is so personal that very few of us can understand the grief involved. Perhaps it will help to ease your sadness if you know that (**name of deceased**) will be greatly missed by all of (**his/her**) friends, and that we all share in your sadness.

(**Name of deceased**) was one of the most charming and warmest (**men/women**) I have ever known. I will never forget (**him/her**). My love is with you.

With sympathy,

Death of Parent or Relative

Dear (**name**),

It was with a saddened surprise that I learned of the death of your (**mother/father/type of relative**). I know that it is always a terrible shock when someone so close to you passes away. (**Name of deceased**) was loved by many and will be missed by all.

I wish to express my heartfelt sympathy and the hope that the kind words of your family and friends will make this difficult time a bit easier to bear.

Most sincerely,

Divorce

Dear (**name**),

I was truly sorry to hear that you and (**name of spouse**) are getting a divorce. While I am not aware of the personal reasons for your decision, I am sure that both of you felt this was the only course of action left for you to take under the circumstances.

I certainly will not be taking any sides in regards to this situation—I have, in fact, written a similar letter to (**name of spouse**)—but I want you to know that I am here should you need any assistance or support.

With love,

Illness or Accident

Dear (**name**),

I can't tell you how sorry I was to hear of your (**illness/accident**). Fortunately, I know that you are generally a very healthy person and, as the saying goes, you can't keep a good (**man/woman**) down. I'm certain that your recovery will be swift and complete.

Please let me know when you are feeling well enough to accept visitors. I have a gift I think you'll enjoy, and I'd love to come by and drop it off.

Your friend,

To Child on Death of Parent/Relative

Dear (**name**),

I know how hard it's been for you lately. I too was very saddened by the passing of your (**type of relative**), (**name**). (**He/she**) was very special to me, and I will always remember (**him/her**) fondly.

I wanted you to know that my thoughts are with you, and that I am here to help you through this trying time.

There's nothing I can say to help ease the pain, but at least I can share in your sadness. Please know that I'll do all that I can to see that you are safe and happy.

With love,

To Child on Death of Pet

Dear (**name**),

I was so sorry to hear about the passing of (**name of pet**). I know how much you loved and cared for (**him/her**), and I wanted you to know that you and

(name of pet) were in my thoughts. Just remember all the great times you had with **(name of pet)**, and realize what a happy life **(he/she)** had with you. I too will remember **(name of pet)** with fondness. **(Name of pet)** was such a good **(type of animal)** that you can be sure **(he/she)** is in **(type of animal)** heaven now.

If there is any way I can help you through this difficult time, please don't hesitate to call me.

With love,

FOUR

Congratulations

Many people simply buy pre-written greeting cards for these occasions. Although this practice has become acceptable in our society, it pales in comparison to a personal message that is written by you.

Achievements are important—and sometimes rare—moments in people's lives, and they should be honored accordingly. The following letters are designed for most congratulatory occasions, and can be either handwritten on your stationery or on a blank greeting card.

Achieving a Personal Goal

Dear (**name**),

Congratulations! All of your hard work has finally paid off! I knew that if anyone could (**type of accomplishment**) it would be you. It takes a great deal of talent, effort, and determination to achieve such a challenging goal, and it's very inspiring to me to see you realize it.

If you have some free time, I'd love to celebrate this wonderful achievement with you. I'll give you a call in the next few days to set something up. Once again, congratulations. I'm very proud of you.

Sincerely,

Graduating High School or College

Dear (**name**),

I was delighted to receive the announcement of your graduation. Congratulations! Graduating from (**high school/college**) is always an exciting time in one's life. You can review the past few years with a proud sense of accomplishment, while looking ahead with anticipation to the challenges that you will soon be facing.

I look forward to hearing all about your new experiences at (**name of college/name of company/ etc.**). I am confident that you will continue to be a success in the years to come. Keep up the good work!

Fondly,

On Anniversary

Dear (**names of husband and wife**),

Happy anniversary! (**Number**) years together is certainly reason to celebrate. The love you two share continues to amaze me. If I didn't know you better, I'd swear that you were newlyweds!

Enjoy this happy occasion, and here's to another (**number**) years together—I hope they are as wonderful as these past years have been.

Best wishes,

On Birth

Dear (**name**),

Congratulations on the birth of your new baby! I am so happy to hear that both mother and child are healthy. There's nothing more exciting than the feeling of bringing a new life into the world.

You and (**name of spouse**) are a lovely couple and I'm sure you will be fantastic parents to (**name of baby**). (**He/she**) is very lucky to have you for (**his/her**) parents. Here's to many years of happiness for all of you.

Affectionately,

On Engagement/Marriage

Dear (**name**),

I can't tell you how thrilled I was to hear of your (**engagement/marriage**)! Congratulations! You certainly were a great "catch" for (**name of fiancée/ spouse**). And I think that (**name of fiancée/spouse**) is the perfect mate for you. The two of you have a bright future to look forward to, and I'm sure you'll make the most of it.

Allow me to give you both my fondest blessing and my best wishes for a long, happy life together.

Love,

On New House

Dear (**name**),

Welcome to your new home! I'm so proud that you finally found a place of your own. I thought I'd help you get started by offering you this lovely (**type of gift**). I hope it fits the decor.

Just think of all the great times you and your family will soon experience there—that's what truly makes a house a home. If you need any help settling in—unpacking, painting, wallpapering, etc., you can always call me.

Best regards,

On New Job

Dear (**name**),

What a pleasant surprise to hear that you're the new (**title**) at (**name of company**). Then again, I'm really not that surprised. You've always impressed me with your talent, work ethic and smarts, and I knew it wouldn't take long for others to notice.

Now it's time to show your new employers what you can *really* do. I can't wait to see the results.

So congratulations on the new job! I can't think of anyone more deserving. Most importantly, I hope you *enjoy* it. Dig in!

Best regards,

On Opening Your Own Business

Dear (**name**),

I just heard that you're finally opening your own business. That's wonderful! I'm so happy for you. I know it's always been your dream to run your own (**type of business**), and it's great to hear that you've made it a reality. No more answering bosses or watching the clock!

Let's celebrate—I'll drop by your (**store or restaurant opening/new office**) and we can toast your future success in person.

Best regards,

On Promotion

Dear (**name**),

Well, I knew it was only a matter of time before your superiors would reward all of your hard work and brilliance with a promotion! Congratulations on your new position! Your skills and smarts will surely serve you well as the new (**name of position/title**).

Best wishes for continued success. I can't wait to see how impressed everyone will be when you start to make a real difference in the (**name of department**) department.

Again, congratulations—you deserve it. I am extremely confident that your future holds many more promotions of such prestige.

Best regards,

On Retirement

Dear (**name**),

Congratulations on your retirement! (**Number**) years as the (**name of position/title**) is quite a long time, and you sure did make the most of it.

I know that, with all of the activities and organizations in which you are involved, your retirement will be a busy one. No loafing around the house for you! Just make sure that you don't work too hard, okay? You deserve some rest and relaxation, as well as the time and freedom to enjoy your "golden years." Stay young!

Love,

To Child on Accomplishment

Dear **(name)**,

I heard that you **(earned an excellent grade/ received a merit badge/performed brilliantly)** in **(school/scouts/type of sport/a show)**, and I wanted to tell you how proud I am of you!

You are a wonderful **(boy/girl)**, and I love you dearly. It's exciting to watch you find your talents and make the most of them. I know this is only the beginning, and I'm looking forward to sharing other important moments with you.

Love,

FIVE

Declining an Invitation

The majority of us, most of the time, are happy to receive invitations. But sometimes we have scheduling conflicts, or we simply choose not to attend for personal reasons. At the same time, we wish to stay in good favor with the person who is extending the invitation.

So a letter declining an invitation should always be polite and respectful. You should express thanks for the invitation, regret for being unable to attend, and offer a brief explanation for your decision. If possible, it's an excellent idea to offer an alternative suggestion for getting together. This will lessen the recipient's disappointment and keep the relationship healthy.

Emergency Came Up

Dear **(name)**,

Please accept my apologies for not attending your **(type of event)** after informing you that I would be coming. As I was preparing to leave that day, **(describe the emergency)**. In the midst of all the turmoil, I simply forgot to telephone you. I hope you'll understand.

(Name of mutual friends) told me that it was a wonderful **(type of event)**, and I'm sorry that I missed it. Let's be sure to get together soon.

Warmest regards,

How About Some Other Time?

Dear **(name)**,

(Dinner/lunch/type of event) next week sounds delightful, but unfortunately I already have a previous commitment. Are you free some other day? How is **(day/date)**?

Write or call me soon so that we can set something up for another time. I can't wait to see you!

Fondly,

Previous Commitment

Dear **(name)**,

Thank you for the lovely invitation to your **(type of event)**. I was indeed honored to be included among your guests to share this special occasion with you. Unfortunately, I have already accepted an invitation to **(type of event)** on that date. I'm so sorry!

I'm sure that your **(type of event)** is going to be a memorable evening for everyone who attends. Please give my regards to all, and thank you for thinking of me.

Kindest regards,

SIX

Declining a Request

It is flattering to be asked a favor or offered an honor. But sometimes it is just not right. This presents a delicate problem, and a well-written letter will serve the purpose of expressing polite regret and maintaining a respectful distance.

As with a letter declining an invitation, you should express thanks (if applicable) for the offer, regret for being unable to comply, and offer a brief explanation for your decision. Again, it's an excellent idea to offer an alternative suggestion, which will lessen the recipient's disappointment and keep the relationship in good standing.

Of a Loan

Dear (**name**),

Thank you for the kindness you expressed in your recent letter. I am very sympathetic to your request to borrow (**amount/item**), but I must decline.

As much as I would like to help, and feel honored that you have asked, I simply cannot afford to part with the (**amount/item**) you need, even though I know that I can trust you to (**repay/return**) it.

I am hoping there is some other way I can be of service. If you ever need to borrow (**alternate item/money at another time when I am on firmer footing**), please feel free to ask.

Sincerely,

Of a Reference

Dear (**name**),

Although I am normally happy to recommend a (**former employee/friend/acquaintance**), I believe that in this case it would be inappropriate to do so, because I simply (**do not know the applicant well enough/could not locate sufficient information**). I know that (**he/she**) was (**employed/a resident of our town**) from (**date**) to (**date**), but offering any character testimony beyond that would be conjecture on my part.

If there is any other way I can be of service, feel free to ask.

Sincerely,

On a Committee Appointment

Dear **(name)**,

Thank you so much for the confidence you have placed in my abilities by nominating me to this respected position, but I feel I must decline.

My current priorities are with my **(job/family/other position)**, and I do not feel I can devote a sufficient amount of time to do the position justice. However, I do hope I can be of service in other ways.

I know you will find a suitable candidate who will bring energy and leadership to the job, and I'll be happy to help in the search.

Again, I am grateful for the generous offer, and I regret that my circumstances prevent me from accepting.

Best regards,

SEVEN

Encouragement and Emotional Messages

The following letters are examples of writing from the heart, either expressing genuine support for a loved one's pending challenge, communicating honest emotions, or simply telling someone you are thinking of them.

This type of thought is often communicated verbally, and that's a shame, because the message will contain an even greater value if it is written. The key is to offer your emotional support genuinely, but realistically. Don't make promises that you can't keep, because in the long run, that will do more harm than good. A combination of a generous spirit and a pragmatic approach is ideal.

Encouragement During Setback

Dear (**name**),

I was truly saddened to hear of your recent misfortune, and I wanted you to know that I am here for you should you need any help or support during this difficult time. I know that things are looking rather bleak at the moment, but you have always shown a tremendous amount of strength and courage, and I'm certain that you will be able to overcome this temporary setback.

For better or worse, we all face a variety of tests in our lives, and I'm confident that you will pass this one with flying colors. There is a light at the end of this dark tunnel—please let me know if there is anything I can do to help you reach it.

Your friend,

For a Homesick Child

Dear (**name**),

We were thrilled to hear from you the other day, but we are concerned about the depth of your homesickness. We miss you too! And I know that your (**brother(s)/sister(s)/friends**) feel the same way. But there will be times during your life that work or school or some other important commitment will take you away from your family and friends. Fortunately, these periods of separation are only temporary, and when you return, you will be a more knowledgeable and mature person.

The holidays will be here sooner than you can imagine, and we will all be together once again. Until then, try to remain focused on your goals and your work, and know that all of us back home are extremely proud of you. Everyone sends their love, and is looking forward to seeing you in the near future.

Love,

Friend's Loss of Job

Dear (**name**),

I'm sure you're feeling unsettled and perhaps a little shaken after your recent setback, but I just wanted to let you know that I'm here to help you through this difficult period. Misfortunes happen to all of us, and you shouldn't take it too hard. You're much too talented to let it hold you back.

In fact, I have already taken the liberty of mentioning your name to a few associates who may be able to help secure you a position with a new company. With someone as qualified as you, it will not take long to get you back on your feet.

If there is anything further I can do, please don't hesitate to call.

Sincerely,

Get Well Soon

Dear (**name**),

I was saddened to hear of your recent illness, and just wanted you to know that I am thinking of you. I know how strong you are, and I have no doubt that your fortitude will help you fully recover very soon.

I am happy to be of service during this difficult time, so if there is anything I can do, please don't hesitate to call.

Sincerely,

Loss of Game or Contest

Dear (**name**),

We just wanted to let you know how proud of you we are for doing your best at (**recent event**). We know you are disappointed, but there will be other (**events/opportunities**). And when you do finally win, you will truly know how to appreciate it. Use this experience as a motivation, and just think how great you'll feel when you're on top.

But ultimately, you can only do your best, and that's what you did at (**recent event**). So hold your head high, and know that we love you.

Affectionately,

Miss You

Dear (**name**),

How are you? Is everything going well? Are you happy? I can't believe that it has been (**length of time**) since you moved away. It seems like it was only yesterday that I could pop over to your house for a quick visit or meet you at (**name of restaurant**) for lunch. How quickly time passes...

I miss you so much! I realize that, because of the distance that separates us, it would be difficult for one of us to visit the other. Perhaps we could take a vacation together at a spot that is halfway between us. Regardless, please write or call soon, our friendship is too special to allow a few miles to put an end to it.

Your friend forever,

On Making Mistakes

Dear (**name**),

I know you feel just awful about what happened at (**the office/the sporting event/the performance, etc.**), but you must put it behind you. It's a cliché, but it's true that we all make mistakes, and no one is perfect.

Every one of us has "blown it"—often seriously—and yet we've still managed to somehow overcome our errors and move on successfully through life.

(Describe a similar event in your life if appropriate.) You will too.

Fondly,

Support for a Performance

Dear **(name)**,

All of us here in **(location)** are very excited about your upcoming **(event)**, and we just wanted to let you know we're behind you one hundred percent.

We've watched you work diligently toward this goal, and have admired your talent, perseverance and determination. You're one of the finest representatives our **(school/city/country)** could have, and we wanted you to know how proud of you we are. You can use our spirit for that extra incentive when the time comes.

Good luck in **(location)**. We know you'll do the very best you can, and we're looking forward to sharing in your success when you return.

Best regards,

EIGHT

Informal Messages for Holidays and Special Occasions

These days, perhaps the highest number of written messages we send are for special occasions. Most of us simply buy pre-written greeting cards for these purposes, but it need not be so. You can either create your own card, write a nice note on your stationery, or write your message on a blank card.

In any case, most of these messages are highly personal, and so these samples are, by necessity, only suggestions. Whenever possible, you should write from your own heart. Use the following samples as guidelines.

Anniversary (Marriage) Wishes

Dear (**name and name of spouse**),

Congratulations on your (**number**) wedding anniversary! It is truly wonderful to watch the both of you go through life so happily together—it gives inspiration to the rest of us! I wish you continued happiness.

Best regards,

Anniversary (Partnership) Wishes

Dear (**name and name of partner(s)**),

Congratulations on the (**number**) anniversary of (**name of business**)! It is truly inspiring to see that the (**number**) of you can turn a dream into a reality, and I consider myself fortunate to know you (**both/all**). As long as you keep up your great work, you'll reach many more milestones in your future. Continued good luck!

Best regards,

Birth Announcement

Dear (**name**),

(**Name of your spouse**) and I are very proud to announce the birth of our new (**son/daughter**), (**full name of child**). (**He/she**) was born on (**date**), at

(time), and weighed **(amount)**. **(Name of mother)** is happy and healthy as well.

We'll be bringing **(name of child)** home soon. We'd love to show **(him/her)** off to you soon after that, so we hope you can make some time for a visit.

Best regards,

Birthday Wishes

Dear **(name)**,

Happy Birthday! I hope this day is happy and memorable for you. You deserve it. **(Mention any other personal remembrance of the past year or statement of support for upcoming year.)**

Love,

Christmas Wishes

Dear **(name)**,

(Name of spouse) and I would like to wish you and **(names of family members)** the best of holidays and a successful **(next year's year)**.

Best regards,

Class Reunion

Dear (**name of alumnus**),

Yes, another (**number**) years have passed, and it's time for the (**number-**) year reunion of (**name of school**)'s class of (**year**). You and a guest are invited to once again relive the past and catch up with all your old friends and classmates.

We'll be holding this event on (**date**) at (**location**), and there will be (**describe theme/type of entertainment/other festivities**).

As soon as we finalize the details, we will send you a detailed invitation, maps, and other information.

If you would like to help us organize this reunion, please contact this year's reunion coordinator, (**name**), at (**address**) or (**telephone number**), by (**date**).

For now, start planning your schedule accordingly, and we hope to see you there!

Sincerely,

Family Reunion

Dear (**name**),

Guess what? (**Name of spouse**) and I thought it was time we gathered the entire (**name of family**) clan together for a family reunion. It has certainly been a long time since we've all seen each other, and of course there are many new additions and much to catch up on.

We'll be having this reunion on **(day)**, **(date)** at **(time)** at **(location)**. **(Name of spouse)** and I only have so much room in our house, but we'll do our best to provide everyone with comfortable quarters, or provide you with any information you need on local accommodations.

For now, let us know if you can make it so we can start planning accordingly. It will be great to see you and **(names of the rest of recipient's family members)** again.

Love,

Father's Day Wishes

Dear **(name of your father)**,

Happy Father's Day! Thanks for all the help you've given me, Dad, throughout the years. You're the best! I hope you enjoy this gift I've sent to you—you deserve it.

Love,

Formal Engagement Announcement

Mr. and Mrs. **(name of bride's parents)**
have the honor of announcing
the engagement of their daughter
(name)
to **(name of groom)**

Optional:
(Name of bride's parents)
request your presence at
(type of event (i.e. luncheon/dinner/reception))
on **(day)**,
(date),
at **(location)**
from **(time)** to **(time)**
to celebrate this happy occasion.

Please R.S.V.P. to **(name)**
at **(telephone number)**
by **(date)**.

Formal Wedding Invitation

Mr. and Mrs. **(name of bride's parents)**
request the honor of your presence
at the marriage of their daughter
(name)
to **(name of groom)**
on **(day)**, **(date (spelled out))**
at **(time (spelled out))**
at **(location)**.

Please R.S.V.P. to **(name)**
at **(telephone number)**
by **(date)**.

Graduation Announcement

Dear **(name)**,

(Name of your spouse) and I are having a little get-together on **(day)**, **(date)**, at **(time)**, at **(location)** to celebrate our **(son/daughter)**'s graduation from **(high school/college)**. We would be delighted if you would help us celebrate.

(Name of son/daughter) has had a wonderful experience at **(name of school)**, and is now moving on to **(name of college/name of company/etc.)** in **(location)**. **(Name of your spouse)** and I are very proud of **(him/her)**.

We hope to see you there.

Best regards,

Mother's Day Wishes

Dear **(name of your mother)**,

Happy Mother's Day! Thank you for all you've done for me. You're the best! I hope you enjoy every moment of this day—you deserve it.

Love,

Valentine's Day Wishes

Dear (**name of your husband/wife/boyfriend/girlfriend**),

How sad that we can't be together on this, our special day. I miss you and love you and wish I could be with you. But since I can't be, I'll just have to wish you a happy Valentine's Day, and wait patiently until the next time I see you so we can celebrate it in style.

Love always,

NINE

Invitations

In writing invitations, clarity and brevity are important. Never be vague with an invitation. If the occasion is formal, present the facts proudly and succinctly. If informal, a little gentle persuasion or a sense of fun will go a long way towards attracting a high turnout of guests.

Baby or Bridal Shower

Dear **(name)**,

As you may already know, **(name)** is **(getting married/having a baby)**, and we've decided to throw a shower for her. Please join us on **(date)** from **(beginning time to ending time)** at **(location)** for the festivities.

We'll be serving refreshments from **(start time)** to **(end time)**.

Please R.S.V.P. to **(name)** at **(number)**. We look forward to seeing you there.

Sincerely,

Benefit Function

Dear **(name)**,

Please join us for **(sponsoring organization)**'s annual benefit **(event)** for **(cause)** on **(day)** evening, the **(date)** of **(month)**, at **(location)**. We will be hosting a reception at **(time)** and dinner at **(time)**, followed by **(describe entertainment)** at **(time)**.

We ask all of our guests to contribute a **(donation/pledge)** of **(amount)** to **(beneficiary)**. We know you understand the importance of the cause, and we truly hope you will be able to attend.

Please return the enclosed reservation with your **(donation/pledge)** to **(name of function coordinator)** by **(date)**.

Respectfully,

Casual Party

Dear (**name**),

I'm having a little get-together at my home to celebrate (**describe occasion**), and I would love it if you could attend. It's a (**theme**) party, so (**contribute a type of food/dress in costume, etc.**), and be prepared to have fun!

This all happens on (**day**), (**date**), from (**time**) to (**time**).

Please R.S.V.P. to (**name**) at (**telephone number**), by (**date**).

Best regards,

For a Child to Join Family Vacation

Dear (**name**),

We have a great idea: we are planning a vacation trip to (**location**) this season, and we would love for you to join us. You and (**name of your son/daughter**) could have a great time together exploring, playing games, and seeing the sights of (**location**).

Of course, we know it's up to your folks to decide whether you can go, and we'll ask them as well, but we'd first like to know if it sounds like fun to you. Think about it, talk to your mom and dad about it, and let us know soon so we can include you in our plans.

We can't wait to hear from you!

Your friends,

Informal Wedding

Dear (**name**),

Please join us on the occasion of the marriage of (**name of bride**) and (**name of groom**), in a private ceremony to be held at (**the home of.../secluded location...**) on (**day**), (**date**). We would be honored if you would share in their happiness and help us celebrate their new life together.

A reception will follow at (**location**).

Please R.S.V.P. to (**name**) at (**telephone number**), by (**date**).

Sincerely,

Overnight Guest

Dear (**name**),

We have been told by our (**mutual friend/relative**) that you will soon be coming to our town, and we would be honored if you would stay with us while you are here.

We feel as if we already know you, having heard so much from (**name of friend/relative**) about you. It would be a great pleasure to show you the sights of (**name of city**).

Please let us know of your arrival time so we can arrange to meet you. We look forward to having you.

Sincerely,

Parents' Permission for Child to Join Family Vacation

Dear **(name)**,

How are you? It's been too long since we last spoke. Of course, you know that **(name of your son/daughter)** and **(name of addressee's child)** are great friends, and we think that's wonderful. We really like **(name of child)**, and always enjoy **(his/her)** company when **(he/she)** is visiting.

In fact, we had an idea: we would love it if **(name of child)** could join us on our upcoming vacation to **(location)**, if you would allow it. We think it would be a great experience for both of our children to visit **(location)** and enjoy an extended visit with each other as well. Of course, we will care for **(name of child)** as if **(he/she)** were our own, and always make sure every precaution is taken for **(his/her)** safety.

(Name of child) has already indicated that **(he/she)** would love to join us, but we know that it is really up to you. Please think it over, and let us know soon so that we can include **(name of child)** in our plans.

We look forward to hearing from you.

Best regards,

Sponsorship

Dear **(name)**,

You may have heard that on **(date)**, **(name of charity/cause)** will be throwing its annual **(dance**

contest/walkathon/etc.) to raise funds. It promises to be a fantastic time, and I will be participating.

I am wondering if you can contribute something to my efforts. I am seeking sponsors for (**amount**) per (**time/mile/etc.**), and I hope to raise at least (**amount**).

I truly believe it's a worthy cause: your contribution will help make a significant difference in the lives of (**name of beneficiaries**). Won't you pledge something? Your support is greatly appreciated. Thank you.

Sincerely,

Surprise Party

Dear (**name**),

Ssshhh... It's a surprise. On (**day/date**), (**name of mutual friend**) will (**turn number of years old/have another birthday**), and we'd like you to share it with (**him/her**).

I've made arrangements for (**mutual friend**) to be out until (**time**), so please arrive at (**earlier time**) sharp so we can all be ready when (**he/she**) arrives.

Please R.S.V.P. to (**name**) at (**telephone number**), by (**date**).

See you there... and mum's the word.

Best regards,

TEN

Reminders and Admonitions

In our busy lives, we often forget the little things. But, of course, those little things can quickly expand and become big problems if not attended to. Look at these sample letters as ways to maintain a healthy relationship.

Also, it is important to carry the right tone with admonitions: be firm, and state clearly what you want, but do not couch it in anger or speak down to the other person. These are simply situations where you should "nip it in the bud" before it balloons into a major disagreement.

Following Through on a Promised Favor

Dear (**name**),

Do you remember that when we last spoke, you offered to (**describe favor**)? Well, I appreciated your offer very much, and thought I'd remind you about it to see if you could make it happen.

It would mean a great deal to me, and your generosity would carry a long way. So do let me know when (**type of favor**) can be arranged, so I can proceed with my plans.

If there is anything I can do in return, please do not hesitate to ask. Thank you.

Best regards,

Offensive Behavior/Foul Language

Dear (**name**),

You are one of our closest friends, someone whom we enjoy having to our home on a regular basis. However, (**name of your spouse**) and I feel that it is necessary to discuss a rather delicate problem with you.

You see, we feel that (**the behavior you displayed/ your use of foul language**) during your last visit to our home was inappropriate considering the number of young children present on this occasion. Additionally, several guests and (**name of your spouse**) and I also found your behavior incredibly offensive.

(Name of friend), we value your friendship very much. Please make an attempt to clean up your act! We know that you are capable of much better behavior.

Sincerely,

Please Return My...

Dear (**name**),

On (**date**) you borrowed my (**name of item**), and told me that you would return it within (**length of time**). Well, it's now been (**length of time**) and I still haven't heard anything from you. I don't mean to be bothersome, but could you please bring my (**name of item**) back to me?

If there is a problem, please call or write to me as soon as possible. Otherwise, I'll expect to see you and my (**name of item**) in the next day or two.

Sincerely,

Repay a Loan

Dear (**name**),

On (**date**) I loaned you (**amount of loan**). At that time you promised that you would pay me back, in full, by (**date**). (**Number of days or weeks**) have now passed since that date, and I haven't heard from you. I don't mean to be bothersome, but I must ask, is there a problem? Please contact me as soon as possible so we can talk about this matter.

If you have already sent the payment, and expected it to reach me by now, you may want to consider placing a stop payment on the check, and then write me another one. If you sent the payment to me within the past few days, then thank you.

I look forward to hearing from you, one way or the other.

Sincerely,

Sharing the Cost of a Gift

Dear (**name**),

As you may recall, we agreed to split the cost of our gift to (**name of recipient**). To that end, I am enclosing a copy of the receipt, and would like you to reimburse me for half of the amount shown, which is (**amount**).

(**Name of recipient**) seemed to really appreciate the (**type of gift**), so it was a worthy choice, and your kindness was appreciated.

Please send me your check as soon as you can.

Sincerely,

To Repair Damage

Dear (**name**),

Enclosed please find an estimate from (**name of repair/cleaning company**) to (**repair/clean**) the damage

(you/your children/your pet) caused to my **(home/yard/type of possession)**. While I realize that you in no way intentionally caused this damage, I think that it is only fair for you to pay for the cost of repairs.

I hope to hear from you soon. Thank you.

Sincerely,

To Telephone Mother or Father

Dear **(name of your sibling)**,

I just thought I'd remind you to call **(mom/dad)** soon. I just spoke to **(him/her)**, and **(he/she)** mentioned that **(he/she)** would love to hear from you too.

I realize that you're quite busy, and I know how easy it is to overlook such things, but family is important. We won't always have each other, so let's make the best of it while we do.

And when you get a chance, call me too. Why don't we get together for dinner soon?

Love,

To Visit an Ailing Relative or Mutual Friend

Dear **(name)**,

As you know, **(name of relative/mutual friend)** is recuperating from **(his/her)** recent **(illness/acci-**

dent). Having just returned from a visit myself, I thought I would remind you of the importance of paying a call.

(**He/she**) spoke of you often, and I believe (**he/she**) would greatly enjoy—and benefit from—seeing you again. I know your schedule is extremely tight, but you can make the time if you try, and it would so brighten (**name of patient**)'s day, as recovery can be such a long and tedious experience. Please call (**name of patient**) soon and let (**him/her**) know you'll be coming. Visiting hours at (**name of hospital**) are (**days**), from (**time**) to (**time**).

If you get a chance, let me know how (**he/she**) is doing after your visit. Thanks.

Sincerely,

ELEVEN

Thank-You Notes

Too often in a situation that calls for a thank-you note, we simply take the lazy way out and send a pre-written card. In fact, a handwritten thank-you note is far more effective, and shows that since you took the time to write it, your appreciation is genuine. Once again, adding your own personal touches to the following samples is always a good idea.

Dinner/Party

Dear (**name**),

I just wanted to drop you a note to tell you how much fun (**name of your spouse**) and I had at your home last night. The (**dinner was absolutely delicious!/party was so much fun!**) You are a terrific host and you have a lovely place.

I'll be sure to reciprocate the invitation the next time I (**have a dinner party/throw a party**). Until then, perhaps we can get together for a night on the town. I'll give you a call real soon. Thanks again!

Best regards,

Favor

Dear (**name**),

Thank you for (**describe favor**). It was really sweet of you to do, and I appreciate it very much. I was stuck in a tough spot and didn't know where else to turn. Thank God you were there for me.

Please, if I can return the favor in any way, shape, or form, do not hesitate to ask. Once again, thank you for your help.

Warmest regards,

Gift

Dear (**name**),

Thank you for the beautiful (**type of gift**)! As usual you have chosen something I most definitely need. Are you a mind reader? You seem to have an incredible talent for always buying the perfect gift!

Whenever I **(look at/use)** it I will think of you and your kindness and generosity.

With much love,

Helping Resolve a Dispute

Dear (**name**),

It was so nice of you to come to our assistance when (**name**) and I were deadlocked in our disagreement, and I just wanted to let you know that your help made the difference in resolving it.

Your patience, unbiased approach, and sympathetic understanding of the situation opened us up to the fundamental truths underlying our positions, and now we are not only communicating again, but doing so with a greater sensitivity to each other. It's wonderful not to be at odds anymore. Thank you so much for your wisdom and wonderful gift for conflict resolution.

If I can ever help in any way, do not hesitate to ask.

Sincerely,

Honesty

Dear (**name**),

I know it took some courage to be honest with me about the problems I was discussing with you, and I want to let you know how much I appreciate the risk you took. Even though the criticism was difficult to swallow at first, I understand that it was for the best. I am already seeing things in a much clearer light, and I believe this will help me change my life for the better.

I asked for your opinion because I respected it, and you delivered. You reminded me that in the long run, it is much more valuable to speak the truth to people, and that hurt feelings are only temporary. Thank you again for making a difference.

Love,

Hospitality

Dear (**name**),

Thank you so much for your hospitality last week. It was extremely nice of you to allow me to stay with you during my visit to (**name of city**). You have a lovely home and a wonderful city and I had a great time. You're an excellent host and I truly appreciate all that you did for me during my stay.

If you ever plan on visiting (**name of your city**), please don't hesitate to call me. As the saying goes, "my house is your house!" I'd love to have you as my guest.

Best wishes,

Information/Suggestion

Dear (**name**),

Thank you for forwarding the information on (**type of service/product/etc.**) that I requested when we last spoke. I will be reviewing the materials with great interest, as I value your recommendation. I'll be calling you soon to discuss the specifics.

Best regards,

Payment of Personal Loan

Dear (**name**),

Thank you for your recent payment of (**amount**). It comes in handy right now, as I need it for (**a down payment on a car/child's college fund/new computer, etc.**) Let me know if there is anything else I can do to help.

Best regards,

Personal Loan

Dear (**name**),

I just want to let you know how much I appreciate you lending me this money. It provides a big help to (**name of your spouse**) and I until we can get on our feet again. Rest assured that we will repay you as soon as we are able to. If there is anything we can ever do for you, please don't hesitate to ask.

Sincerely,

Personal Introduction

Dear (**name**),

I just wanted to thank you for introducing me to your (**friend/relative**), (**name**). (**He/she**) and I have become fast friends, and have been greatly enjoying getting to know each other. (**He/she**) has become a wonderful addition to my life, and it's because of you. Thank you again, and I hope I can return the favor.

Best regards,

Recommendation

Dear (**name**),

Thank you very much for the letter of recommendation you sent on my behalf to (**name of person or company**). I know how busy you are, and I truly appreciate your taking the time to do this for me. (**Name of person or company**) values your opinion, and your recommendation was a large factor in my landing the job.

I will do my best and work as hard as I possibly can to live up to the words of praise you conveyed about me.

With much gratitude,

Support, Encouragement, or Advice

Dear (**name**),

What can I say? You're the best. When I was down, you (**offered words of support/encouraged me/gave me advice**) that helped to lift me up out of my doldrums. Because of you, I have now seen the light, and my life is back on track.

It's difficult to express how much the fact that you simply cared has meant to me. You were there when I needed you, and I want you to know that I will always be there for you—any time, any day. You are a true friend, and I value our relationship to no end.

Love,

Sympathy

Dear (**name**),

Thank you for your kind expression of sympathy upon the death of (**name**). Your warm words provided a tremendous amount of strength and support to me during this difficult time. I know that (**name of deceased**) valued your friendship, and that (**he/she**) would be grateful for all of the nice things you had to say about (**him/her**).

I hope that we will be able to get together some time in the near future. I have a few items of (**name of deceased**)'s that I am sure (**he/she**) would have liked you to have.

Sincerely,

To a Child for Thinking of...

Dear (**name**),

Thank you so much for your (**card/gift**)! It was very thoughtful of you to remember (**name of recipient**)'s (**type of occasion**), and (**he/she/we**) enjoyed it very much. You are a kind, loving person, and you certainly showed it on this occasion. We're very proud to have you as a (**friend/type of relative**). Hopefully, we'll come visit you soon so we can thank you in person.

Fondly,

Volunteering on a Fundraiser

Dear (**name**),

I want to thank you for donating your valuable time and effort to pitch in during (**name of project or organization**)'s recent (**benefit/event**). Your contribution helped us reach our goal—we raised (**amount**)!

I also hope you enjoyed the experience—everyone seemed to appreciate your efforts, and we certainly all had a good time. Can we count on you next year?

Best of luck with your (**personal/career goals discussed**), and I look forward to seeing you again.

Sincerely,

Business Letters

Business letters serve two main purposes: first, they open the lines of communication to help you receive a desirable response, whether it's solving a problem, making arrangements, or seeking information; and second, they serve as official records of correspondence, so that you can strengthen your case, if need be, with physical proof.

It is vitally important that you follow a few simple rules when writing business letters. Doing so will allow you to capture the attention of the recipient and enable you to get what you want.

- Imagine yourself in the position of the recipient. You have a stack of mail on your desk and you don't have the time or, frankly, the inclination to read and answer each and every letter. Which do you respond to? The one that is addressed "To Whom It May Concern" and is sloppily written, or the one that is addressed to you personally, formatted neatly, and communicated respectfully and effectively?

- Today's business world is technologically advanced—virtually every type of office is computerized. But the people who run these offices are still very much human beings, so the traditional rules of effective letter writing, with a respectful human touch, still apply. In fact, it could be argued that in an increasingly automated world, it is even more important to emphasize our human qualities.

Where Should I Turn for Help?

When writing a letter to resolve a business matter, try to address it to the person with whom you have already been in contact. This person will usually be familiar with your situation; or if not, will probably be in a "hands-on" position, and will be able to expedite the matter most quickly.

If this fails, then and only then should you go a step higher—to that person's supervisor, or as the case may be, from a local to a regional or national office.

Other Guidelines:

- Get to the point! Respect the time of the recipient, and don't burden him or her with rambling or secondary background information. State your reason for writing in your first paragraph and stay on track.

- Always include facts that will help ease the recipient's task. For instance, if you are writing to a bank, mention your account number early so that he will not have to look it up.

- If you refer to other correspondence, mention those by date, check number, etc. Include copies whenever possible.

- Always be courteous! Even if you are frustrated or angry, maintaining a cool, calm approach will be beneficial to your situation.

The Format

Use the following as a guideline to writing an effective business letter:

Return address

Today's date

Name of recipient
Recipient's title
Name of company, organization, or institution
Street address or post office box
City, state, zip code

Opening salutation:

Body of letter

Conclusion

Closing salutation,

(allow four returns here)

Your signature
Your name
CC:
Enclosure:

Now Let's Discuss Each Step Specifically

Return Address. If you have pre-printed stationery, there is no need to include a return address at the top of your letter. However, if you do not, you must include this information at the very top (note: use only your address—your name still goes under your signature at the bottom). Never expect the recipient to find your address on the envelope, as it is often discarded upon opening.

Today's Date. Dating your letter, and dating it in a clear manner, is crucial. Always completely spell out the month. Use actual numbers for the date and year. For example, May 14, 2001.

Recipient's Name and Address. As stated above, the person to whom you are sending the letter will always choose to read and answer a letter addressed specifically to him before one with a generic greeting, for instance, "Dear Sir" or "Gentlemen."

So how do you find out the name of the best person to whom to address your letter? Just call the company or organization, explain the nature of your inquiry as concisely as possible to the receptionist, and ask for the name of the person to whom you should address the letter. If you are courteous and pleasant on the phone, most receptionists will be more than happy to give you this information. If you run into a problem, however, you should ask to speak to the receptionist's supervisor, or to someone in the Human Resources department.

If you know the person's title, then it will be helpful to include that under their name, but before their company name.

Opening Salutation. The easiest and most proper forms of salutations are simply "Dear Mr. (name)" for a man, and "Dear Ms. (name)" for a woman. For official titles, consult the "Forms of Address" glossary at the back of the book. Remember to never use a first name only (i.e., "Dear Lucia,") unless you already know the person well. Follow your greeting with a colon (i.e., "Dear Mr. Baker:").

Body of the Letter. As you can see, the format page above is in "full-block" style, with all paragraphs flush left. Allow a full space between the paragraphs. All business letters should be typed or printed from a computer.

It is important to organize your thoughts carefully. The more coherent and structured your letter, the more impressive your statement. Be brief and get right to the point. Report facts accurately, without exaggeration or hyperbole. The recipient of your letter will appreciate your consideration of her time, as well as your respect for her intelligence. The letters in this book follow these rules. Use them as is, but learn from them at the same time.

Conclusion. You will notice that at the end of almost every sample business letter contained in this book, a "thank you" appears before the closing. It can be placed at the end of the body of the letter, or in a separate paragraph by itself. This show of gratitude is not only a sign of common decency, but also a subtle nudge towards a response that will ultimately benefit you. "Thank you for your assistance" not only expresses appreciation, it subtly rewards the recipient for the efforts she is about to make on your behalf.

Closing Salutation. Since this is a business letter, it is important that your closing reflect a respectful distance. Never assume anything more! Therefore, informal closings such as "Fondly," "Best regards," or "Yours truly" are inappropriate.

In nearly every case, a simple "Sincerely" will do just fine.

Always leave at least four line spaces for your signature, under which your name will appear typed. You may also include additional information below your name. It is appropriate, for instance, in a letter to the I.R.S. to include your Social Security number beneath your name.

CC. In the old days, "CC" stood for "carbon copies,." and thus referred to those people to whom a copy of your letter would be sent. Although almost no one uses carbon copies anymore, the meaning of "CC" remains the same.

You may not use this that often. But if you deemed it wise to send a copy of your letter to another person, such as your attorney, your recipient's attorney, your physician, the recipient's supervisor, etc., you would place those names in list format after the "CC:"—remember your full colon!

Enclosure. In many cases, you will need to support your position with copies of original documents. For instance, if you are writing to a bank to dispute a charge on your statement, you will need to enclose a copy of that statement. You would then type "Enclosure: Statement for checking account number (**your account number**)."

TWELVE

Banking and Credit

In today's world, a good credit rating has taken on a role of major importance. It's a record of your financial reliability, and so it should be protected and carefully guarded.

This becomes even more important when you consider that, because they handle so many accounts and process so many transactions, banks and credit institutions will make mistakes. So it's up to you to make sure your statements are accurate.

If you notice a problem, don't shrug it off—write a letter to solve the problem. In these cases, a letter is far more powerful than a phone call, because it serves as a permanent record, and allows you to include copies of other materials, such as receipts and statements, to prove your case.

The following are examples of the most common banking, credit and financial situations.

Closing Bank Account—Poor Service

Dear (**name of customer service representative**):

Please close my (**type of account**) account, effective immediately. After complaining repeatedly about inaccuracies and discrepancies on my statements and receiving little or no response, I have no choice but to take my banking elsewhere.

I understand that the current balance on my (**type of account**) account is (**amount**). Please send a check for that amount to the address above to zero out the account. Thank you very much.

Sincerely,

Closing Credit Account

Dear (**name of customer service representative**):

Please close my credit account, (**account number**). I have enclosed my credit cards and a check for (**amount**) to cover what I understand to be the outstanding balance.

I have contacted your accounting department repeatedly about (**inaccuracies/discrepancies**) on my account, but my statements still do not reflect an adequate correction of the problem. I cannot afford to continue doing business amid this confusion, as I am concerned that it could have a negative effect on my credit rating. Therefore, I must terminate my account immediately. Thank you for your understanding.

Sincerely,

Collection Agency Response

Dear (**name of collection agency representative**):

In response to your inquiry, dated (**date**), I am enclosing a copy of my canceled check to (**name of original creditor**), dated (**date**), which you will notice was sent prior to the date of your correspondence, and which satisfies my balance with (**name of original creditor**).

I am also sending the same copy to (**name of original creditor**), along with a copy of this letter, and requesting that they adjust my account accordingly and withdraw any claim that your agency may have on me.

Please acknowledge that you have indeed received this, and that the account from your agency has been withdrawn. I also expect a similar response from (**name of original creditor**), acknowledging that I no longer owe this amount to them. Thank you for your prompt attention to this matter.

Sincerely,

Deposit Not Received

Dear (**name of customer service representative**):

On (**date**), I sent a check in the amount of (**amount**) to you. However, in my most recent statement, dated (**date**), my payment is not reflected.

Enclosed please find a copy of my canceled check, which you deposited on (**date**). Please credit my account, (**number**), in the amount of (**amount**). I trust that any finance charges I have accrued as a result of your oversight will be reversed.

I look forward to seeing the correct totals on my next statement.

Sincerely,

Increase of Credit Limit

Dear (**name of customer service representative**):

I have been a (**cardholder/store credit customer**) for (**number**) years now, and I believe my credit standing with you is in fine order. My overall credit rating is also excellent.

My current credit limit is (**amount**), as it has been for (**length of time**). However, in light of the above, I am requesting that you raise my limit to (**amount**).

Along with my good credit history, my current financial profile is also healthy, so I anticipate no problems assuming the added responsibility of a higher limit.

My primary interest in raising the limit is to improve my credit rating.

Thank you in advance for your favorable consideration of this matter.

Sincerely,

Protesting Charges for Insufficient Funds

Dear (**name of bank manager**):

According to my checking account statement for (**month**), on (**date**) I was charged (**amount**) for insufficient funds. Apparently, check number (**number**) was not honored.

However, my records show that there was indeed sufficient money in the account to cover the check. According to my statement of (**previous month**), my books are in accord with yours, and I have accounted for each check written since (**number of allegedly bounced check**). Furthermore, I have written no checks since then that would explain the discrepancy.

Please contact me at (**telephone number**) immediately about this problem, so that we may ascertain where the error occurred. If I am at fault, I would like to straighten my books as soon as possible to avoid any further problems. If the error is indeed yours, please adjust my account accordingly, reimbursing me for any charges falsely incurred from both your institution and the payee, and inform me of the status of the check in question.

Thank you for your prompt attention to this matter.

Sincerely,

Protesting Service Charges

Dear (**name of bank manager**):

According to my most recent (**type of account**) account statement, dated (**date**), I was charged (**amount**). However, it is my belief that this is an error.

When I opened my account on (**date**), I was informed that if I kept my balance above (**amount**), no service charges would be applied. Yet this statement clearly shows that my balance has indeed remained above the minimum, so I maintain that the charges should be withdrawn.

Please credit my account for (**amount**), the amount of the service charge, and please assure me that no such error will occur in the future. If I am misinformed, please contact me at (**telephone number**) and explain the situation further. Thank you for your prompt attention.

Sincerely,

Request for Credit Report from a Credit Bureau

Dear (**name of credit manager**):

On (**date**) I was denied credit by (**name of credit card/bank/store/etc.**). The creditors based their decision on a credit report provided by your bureau. In accordance with the Fair Credit Reporting Act, I am entitled to see a copy of my credit report, free of charge, in order to check its accuracy.

My complete name is (**your legal name**). My Social Security number is (**Social Security number**). My current address is (**current address**). My former address is (**former address**). Please send my free copy of my credit report to the following address: (**Your name and address**).

Thank you for your prompt attention.

Sincerely,

Request for a Replacement Credit Card

Dear (**name of customer service representative**):

On (**date**), I discovered that my (**type of card**), the account number of which is (**account number**), was missing. I reported this occurrence to your institution on that same date.

My last transaction was on (**date**), for (**amount**). Any charges incurred on this card from that point on must be considered fraudulent. I understand that, according to your cardholder terms, I will not be responsible for any such charges.

Please acknowledge that the account attached to my missing card has indeed been terminated, and please issue me a new card on a new account as quickly as possible.

Thank you for your speedy assistance in this matter.

Sincerely,

Requesting a Current Statement

Dear (**name of bank manager**):

I have a (**type of account**) account at your bank, the number of which is (**account number**). I would appreciate it very much if you could send a current statement reflecting the amount in my account to my above address.

Thank you for your cooperation.

Sincerely,

Requesting Explanation for Denial of Loan

Dear (**name of credit manager**):

Thank you for responding to my application for credit at your (**financial institution/store**). However, I must respectfully ask that you reconsider your decision to deny my application.

You cited in your letter, dated (**date**), that my request was denied based on unfavorable credit information obtained through an inquiry to (**name of agency**).

I was surprised by this explanation, since it is my understanding that my credit rating and existing accounts are in excellent standing. Therefore, I made my own inquiry to (**name of agency**), and discovered that indeed an error had occurred in my file. They have since issued a letter confirming this mistake, and I have enclosed a copy of it for your files.

It is my belief that, based on this new information, you will receive no further unfavorable responses regarding my payment history. Since the error was not my fault, I hope that you will give this new evaluation high priority and expedite my application. Thank you for your prompt attention to this matter.

Sincerely,

Requesting Information on Opening a Bank Account

Dear (**name of customer service representative**):

I am interested in opening a (**type of account**) account, and would like to know the general terms your financial institution offers.

I would like to initially deposit (**amount**), and I anticipate adding approximately (**amount**) on a (**weekly/**

monthly) basis thereafter. Please advise me of your interest rate options and any service fees contingent to a (**type of account**) account.

Thank you for your assistance.

Sincerely,

Requesting a Loan

Dear (**name of bank manager/loan officer**):

Thank you for spending the time discussing my interest in obtaining a (**type of loan**) loan from your financial institution on (**date**). To that end, I have enclosed a completed application. As you may recall, I am planning to use the loan for (**buying a new car/starting a new business/purchasing a new home, etc.**)

If it would be helpful to provide you with any additional information, please do not hesitate to call me at (**telephone number**).

Thank you for your prompt attention to this matter.

Sincerely,

THIRTEEN

Career

If ever strong letter writing skills are needed, it is here in the career category. Very seldom will you write a letter more important than one that concerns your job. A letter written to a supervisor or co-worker will reflect many things about your character, including your intelligence, attention to detail and your passion for the job. Always go over such letters with a fine tooth comb, checking for spelling, grammar and tone. Remember, your success with the company could eventually depend upon your ability to communicate effectively.

Accepting a New Job

Dear (**name of hiring supervisor**):

Thank you for your letter of (**date**), offering me the position of (**title**). I am proud to accept your offer, and I have enclosed a signed copy of the accompanying contract, which reflects a few minor provisions. If there are any problems with these provisions, please call me directly at (**telephone number**), and I will be happy to work them out with you.

Otherwise, as I mentioned during our last interview, I will arrive in (**name of city**) on (**date**), and I will report to you on the morning of (**date**). I am looking forward to joining (**name of company**), and I anticipate great success ahead. Thank you for your courtesy and encouragement during the hiring process—your confidence in me will be rewarded. I'll see you on (**date**).

Sincerely,

Asking for Maternity Leave

Dear (**name of supervisor**):

As you know, I am expecting a child soon; therefore, I am requesting a maternity leave of absence for (**length of time**), which will begin on (**date**). I am enclosing a copy of my doctor's report for your files. I anticipate leaving on (**date**) and returning on (**date**).

If you have any concerns, I will be happy to meet with you to discuss them. I also understand that it may be necessary for me to train a replacement employee to cover my responsibilities while I am away, and I am happy to do so.

Thank you for your understanding of my situation and prompt consideration of my request.

Sincerely,

Asking for a Personal Leave of Absence

Dear (**name of supervisor**):

It has become necessary for me to take time off from my job for personal reasons. I am therefore requesting a leave of absence for (**length of time**), due to (**describe medical reasons/school, etc.**), which will begin on (**date**).

I am enclosing a copy of (**doctor's report/school information, etc.**) to help explain the necessity for my time away. I anticipate leaving on (**date**) and returning on (**date**).

If you have any concerns or objections, I will be happy to meet with you to discuss them. I also understand that it may be necessary for me to train a replacement employee to cover my responsibilities while I am away, and I am happy to do so.

Thank you for your understanding of my situation and prompt consideration of my request.

Sincerely,

Asking for a Raise

Dear (**name of supervisor**):

As you know, it has been (**length of time**) since my last favorable review. Since then, I have continued to prove my value to (**name of company**) in a variety of ways: (**Describe positive contributions**). I appreciate your noticing these contributions, and now I wish to respectfully request consideration for a salary increase.

I enjoy my job very much, and I look forward to continuing my contributions, and perhaps increasing my value to the company. However, with the cost of living continuing to rise, I feel that it is only fair to ask to be compensated for my job performance accordingly.

Thank you for your time and consideration on this matter.

Respectfully,

Asking for a Transfer

Dear (**name of supervisor/personnel director**):

It has come to my attention that the position of (**title**) is opening up at the (**branch/area location**) of (**name of company**), and I would very much like to be considered for that position.

I have been employed by (**name of company**) for (**length of time**) now at the (**location**) office, and I believe the skills and experience I have gained here could benefit the company greatly in this new position. My previous qualifications are also relevant: prior to joining (**name of company**), I was (**title**) at (**name of previous company**), which enabled me to perfect my skills at (**type of job**).

I am also interested in transferring to this area of the company because (**describe other ways the job will benefit you personally**).

I have discussed the possibility of this transfer with my current supervisor, (**name of supervisor**), and (**he/she**) has kindly offered to recommend me for the position.

I am eager to discuss the possibilities with you further, so please contact me at your earliest convenience at (**telephone number**) so that we may arrange a meeting.

Thank you for your consideration.

Sincerely,

Cover Letter for Requested Resumé

Dear (**name of supervisor/personnel manager**):

It was nice speaking with you on (**date**) about the openings in your (**company/department**). As promised, I am enclosing my resumé, which outlines my professional experience, education, and references for your consideration.

I am confident I can make a valuable contribution to (**name of company**), not only with my skills, but also with a high degree of enthusiasm, energy, and reliability.

I am eager to meet with you personally to discuss the possibilities, so please contact me at your earliest convenience so that we may arrange a meeting.

Thank you very much for your time and consideration.

Sincerely,

Cover Letter for Responding to a Classified Ad

Dear (**name of contact given/"Sir or Madam"**):

Enclosed please find a copy of my resumé, which I am submitting to you in response to your advertisement in the (**date**) edition of (**name of publication**) for the position of (**type of position**).

I believe my qualifications are well-suited to the requirements you mentioned in the ad: I am (**describe work values and skills**), and as a result, I am confident that I can make a genuine contribution to (**name of company**).

I am eager to meet with you to discuss the particulars of the position, so please contact me at your earliest convenience so that we may arrange a meeting. You may contact me at the address or phone number listed above.

Thank you for your consideration and response to my inquiry.

Sincerely,

Declining a Job

Dear (**name of executive offering the job**):

Thank you very much for your kind letter of (**date**), offering me the position of (**title**) at your company.

I am very flattered that you have decided to offer me the position. Unfortunately, however, I deeply regret that I will not be able to accept it.

In the period of time that followed my interview with you, I continued to explore other opportunities in the area, and I was fortunate enough to be offered a position with another company, which I accepted.

(**Name of company whose job you are declining**) has an excellent reputation, so I am quite sure you will have no problem filling the position with a highly-qualified candidate.

Thank you again for demonstrating your confidence in my abilities, and best of luck to you and your company in the future.

Sincerely,

Job Inquiry—General

Dear (**name of department supervisor/personnel director**):

I am interested in exploring the possibility of employment at (**name of company**). To this end, I have enclosed a copy of my resumé, which outlines my professional experience, education, and references for your consideration.

As you may notice, I am particularly skilled at (**describe area of expertise**). I am confident I could easily adapt to (**name of company**)'s environment, as I would bring to the company not only these skills, but also a high degree of enthusiasm, energy, and reliability.

If you currently have any openings for which my qualifications would apply, or foresee any in the near future, please contact me at your earliest convenience. I would be eager to meet with you personally to discuss the possibilities.

Thank you very much for your time and consideration.

Sincerely,

Job Inquiry—Reentering Job Market

Dear (**name of department supervisor/personnel director**):

I am interested in exploring the possibility of employment at (**name of company**). To this end, I have enclosed a copy of my resumé, which outlines my professional experience, education, and references for your consideration.

As you may notice, I have been absent from the work force for (**length of time**), during which time I (**traveled/studied/raised children, etc.**) However, I have taken great care to maintain my skills. In fact, during this time I have actually (**broadened/sharpened**) my knowledge of (**field of interest**).

In my previous stint as (**title**) at (**name of last company**), I was valued very highly for my skills and contributions. Therefore, I am confident I could easily adapt to (**name of addressee's company**)'s environment, as I would bring to the company not only these skills, but also a high degree of enthusiasm, energy, and reliability.

If you currently have any openings for which my qualifications would apply, or foresee any in the near future, please contact me at your earliest convenience. I would be eager to meet with you personally to discuss the possibilities.

Thank you very much for your time and consideration.

Sincerely,

Job Inquiry—Relocation

Dear (**name of department supervisor/personnel director**):

I am considering relocating to (**name of city**), and there fore I am also exploring new employment opportunities. I am currently employed as a (**type of position**) at (**name of company**) in (**name of city**), (**name of state**).

I am very interested in the possibility of employment at (**name of company**). To this end, I have enclosed a copy of my resumé, which outlines my professional experience, education, and references for your consideration.

As you may notice, I am particularly skilled at (**describe area of expertise**). In fact, my current employer has kindly agreed to write a letter of recommendation for me, which I have also enclosed. You will find that I have been evaluated highly not only for my skills, but also my enthusiasm, energy, and reliability. As a result, I am confident I could easily adapt to (**name of company**)'s environment, and make a valuable contribution.

If you currently have any openings for which my qualifications would apply, or foresee any in the near future, please contact me at your earliest convenience. I would be eager to meet with you personally to discuss the possibilities.

Thank you very much for your time and consideration.

Sincerely,

Protesting Termination

Dear (**name of company head/personnel grievance administrator**):

On (**date**), I was notified by (**name of supervisor**) that (**name of company**) had decided to terminate my employment, effective (**date**). I was told that (**describe the reasons that were given**).

However, I do not believe I was given a fair chance to respond to these allegations. As you know, termination can damage one's reputation and one's chances of successfully securing employment elsewhere. Therefore, I am seeking a hearing with you **(and/or other parties involved in such disputes, such as a grievance committee)** to present my side of the story.

I believe my high job performance evaluations in prior reviews will show that my termination was unjustified, and possibly manipulated by unprofessional motives.

If you choose not to grant me this hearing, I will have no choice but to take other avenues to protect my reputation and position.

Thank you for your prompt attention to this matter, and I look forward to hearing from you.

Respectfully,

Requesting a Recommendation Letter

Dear **(name of current or former employer/civic leader/colleague/friend)**:

I am currently seeking new employment at **(name of company/companies)**, and I would greatly appreciate it if you could take a few minutes to write a letter of recommendation on my behalf.

The type of work I am seeking involves (**describe qualities**), so it would be particularly helpful if you tailored the letter to that specific area.

I am certain that, with your blessing, my application will be regarded favorably, and I will do my best to justify your confidence in me.

Thank you in advance for this kindness, and please do not hesitate to call me if there is ever anything I can do for you.

Sincerely,

Resignation

Dear (**name of supervisor**):

Please consider this letter as official notice of my intention to resign my position as (**title**) from (**name of company**), effective (**date**).

I do wish to assure you that my reasons for resigning are entirely personal, and not meant to cast aspersions on the company in any way. I have enjoyed my experience here, and I have broadened and sharpened my skills as a result. I have also appreciated the opportunity to work with a talented group of people.

I wish all of you and (**name of company**) best of luck in the future.

I am currently seeking new employment at (**name of company/companies**), and I would greatly appreciate it if you could take a few minutes to write a letter of recommendation on my behalf.

The type of work I am seeking involves (**describe qualities**), so it would be particularly helpful if you tailored the letter to that specific area.

I am certain that, with your blessing, my application will be regarded favorably, and I will do my best to justify your confidence in me.

Thank you in advance for this kindness, and please do not hesitate to call me if there is ever anything I can do for you.

Sincerely,

Thank You for the Job Interview

Dear (**name of interviewer**):

It was very kind of you to take the time from your busy schedule to meet with me on (**date**) to discuss the opening for (**type of position**). I want you to know I appreciated the opportunity.

The meeting certainly increased my interest in the position, which was already high. I was very impressed with your (**describe specifics of the department/company**). I firmly believe I can contribute significantly to the company with my (**describe skills and work values**).

Thank you again for your time and interest in my qualifications, and I look forward to hearing from you about the results of my interview.

Sincerely,

Thank You for the Recommendation

Dear (**name of current or former employer/civic leader/colleague/friend**):

Thank you so much for your kind letter of recommendation on my behalf to (**name of new employer**) at (**name of company**). It proved so effective that I was offered the job of (**type of position**) that I was seeking, over several other highly qualified candidates.

I greatly appreciate this favor, and I will do my best to justify your confidence in me.

Thank you again, and if there is anything I can do at some point to return the favor, feel free to call.

Sincerely,

FOURTEEN

Government

Each time an election rolls around, we hear the same frustrations: Nobody votes anymore... It's the lesser of two evils... I just don't care... What difference can I make?

Sometimes we forget that this is a democracy, governed by and for the people. Obviously, voting is priority number one. But you can also make a difference by writing letters.

There's an old adage that the squeaky wheel gets the grease. If you can write a cogent, thoughtful, respectful letter to a politician, you too will get a response, and you will have made an impact on his or her policy. In turn, you'll begin to think that you do indeed have a voice in your government.

As in most business letters, the more localized the target the better. So if you are concerned with a problem on a local level, write your local representative—he or she is more accessible, more sensitive to the problem, and receives less letters than a national representative.

However, there are times and situations when it is just as important to write to senators, governors, and even the president. By following the same guidelines, you too will be heard.

Encouraging a Politician to Support an Issue

Dear (**name of politician**):

The purpose of this letter is to voice my support of (**describe issue**). I know that it is currently under a great deal of scrutiny, and if certain politicians have their way, it could be dealt a severe—if not fatal—(**financial/constitutional/political**) blow.

(Describe the situation, and your position/suggestions for resolving it.)

I implore you to use your voice in Congress to do anything and everything you can to stave off legislation that would (**cut federal funding/outlaw a practice, etc.**) It's vital that we protect our (**rights/resources, etc.**), and the prospect of a future without this protection is downright frightening.

Sincerely,

Opposing a Politician's Position

Dear (**name of politician**):

I am writing in opposition to your stand on (**describe the issue**). I believe that (**state your position**).

I find it hard to fathom that the voters who put you in office are in agreement with you on this issue. I urge you to reconsider your position on this matter. I appreciate your consideration of my letter.

Sincerely,

Proposing Additional Police to Politician

Dear (**name of politician**):

I wish to register my support for additional police officers in the city of (**name of city**).

As you may already know, the crime rate has been increasing dramatically here, particularly in the neighborhood of (**name of neighborhood**), and those of us who live here are deeply concerned for our safety. My family and I, for instance, are afraid to leave the house at night. In fact, on (**date**), (**describe a particular occurrence**).

It is simply unacceptable to live in this country under these circumstances; therefore, we must take serious action to cut down on the crime here. I am enclosing a petition signed by (**number**) residents of (**name of city**) supporting this position.

I implore you to use your influence in (**Congress/the Senate/city hall, etc.**) to ensure that this measure is approved as quickly as possible. Thank you for your attention to my concerns.

Sincerely,

Proposing Fixing Pothole to Local Politician

Dear **(name of politician)**:

I am writing to you about my concern for the safety of the motorists and cyclists who traverse **(name of street)** in **(name of city)** on a daily basis. There are several potholes on this street that are in desperate need of repair, so much so that they have become a serious safety hazard.

I have enclosed a copy of a petition signed by **(number)** residents in this area, all of whom feel just as strongly about repairing these obstacles as I do.

I understand that the city's budget is tight, but public safety should be our number one priority, and the cost of these repairs is relatively small. The benefit to the public, however, is great.

I implore you to use your influence in city hall to see that this work be approved as quickly as possible. Thank you for your attention to my concerns.

Sincerely,

Proposing a Traffic Light to Local Politician

Dear **(name of politician)**:

I am writing to you about my concern for the safety of the pedestrians and motorists at the intersection of

(name of street) and **(name of street)** in **(name of city)**. I believe it is time to install a traffic light there, for the following reasons.

As you know, the number of residents and businesses in the surrounding area has grown significantly over the last few years, which has resulted in a dramatic increase in traffic flow at this intersection. It has also resulted in a number of traffic accidents and close calls, and it has become particularly dangerous for children.

Installing a traffic light would greatly reduce the hazard of the intersection, and calm the fears of those of us who have children in this neighborhood. I have enclosed a copy of a petition signed by **(number)** residents in this area, all of whom support the idea of a traffic light at the intersection.

I understand that the city's budget is tight, but public safety should be our number one priority, and installing a traffic light at the intersection of **(name of street)** and **(name of street)** is long overdue.

I implore you to use your influence in city hall to see that this measure is approved as quickly as possible. Thank you for your attention to my concerns.

Sincerely, .

Supporting a Politician's Position

Dear **(name of politician)**:

I would like to express my support for your position on **(describe the issue)**. I believe that **(state your position)**. Please let me know if there is anything I can do to **(help this bill pass/further this cause)**.

I appreciate the attention you have given this letter.

Sincerely,

FIFTEEN

Housing

This section is for those housing situations that require a well-written letter, whether it be the resolution of a maintenance problem, closing a sale, warning a tenant, or complaining about a neighbor.

Most housing issues can be divided into three categories: Buying or owning your own home, renting a house or apartment from a landlord, or renting a house or apartment as a landlord. All three situations will be addressed below.

Offer to Purchase a House

Dear (**name of real estate agent/broker**):

Please consider this letter our official notice of intent to purchase the (**house/condominium**) at (**address**) in (**name of city**), (**name of state**), for the previously agreed price of (**amount**).

Thank you for your assistance in finalizing this purchase, and we look forward to a bright future in our new home.

Sincerely,

Withdrawing an Offer to Purchase a House

Dear (**name of real estate agent/broker**):

Please consider this letter as official notice of our intent not to purchase the house at (**address**) in (**name of city**), (**name of state**). We have reconsidered our options, and have decided that this particular residence is not suited for us at this time.

We understand that the current owners have not yet finalized our initial offer, so there should be no problem withdrawing the offer.

Thank you for your assistance in this matter.

Sincerely,

Withdrawing an Offer to Sell a House

Dear (**name of real estate agent/broker**):

Please consider this letter as official notice of our intent not to sell our house at (**address**) in (**name of city**), (**name of state**). We hereby terminate any previous contracts with you in this regard.

Thank you for your efforts in helping us attempt to sell the house. However, we have changed our plans, and no longer wish to list the house for sale at this time.

Sincerely,

Complaining to Landlord about Neighbors

Dear (**name of landlord/property manager**):

As a tenant in good standing of (**address/name of apartment building**), in unit number (**number**), I feel justified in registering a formal complaint about my neighbor in apartment number (**number**). For the past (**length of time**), (**he/she/they**) (**has/have**) been causing me a great deal of disturbance by (**describe specific nature of offense: playing music too loud, annoying late-night guests, littering common areas, etc.**)

I have made repeated attempts to try to allay this behavior, but to no avail. I have also spoken to my other neighbors about this problem, and they too have expressed frustration over the situation and have tried to stop it.

But it appears our efforts are ineffective. Even after my latest discussion with (**name of offensive neighbor**), (**he/she/they**) still proceeded to (**describe disturbance**) just last (**day**).

I implore you to contact (**this/these tenant(s)**) and insist that they stop this behavior. I am sure that if the edict comes from you, it will be far more effective.

Thank you for your help and understanding.

Sincerely,

Notice of Intent to Leave

Dear (**name of landlord/property manager**):

This letter is to hereby inform you that I intend to vacate apartment number (**number**) at (**address**) on (**date**). As you recall, when I initially moved in, I paid the amount of (**amount**) as a security deposit. According to the rental agreement, I should receive that amount back no later than (**number**) days after the date of my departure.

I have enjoyed my term of residence here. My decision to leave is personal, and in no way reflects negatively on the quality of the apartment.

Please send my deposit to my new address, (**address**). If you need to contact me for any additional reasons,

I can be reached at (**telephone number**) until (**date**); after that, my new number will be (**telephone number**).

Thank you for your cooperation.

Sincerely,

Protesting Monthly Rent Increase

Dear (**name of landlord/property manager**):

Recently, I was notified of your intention to increase my monthly rent from (**amount**) to (**amount**).

I must respectfully protest this increase, based on the following:

First, I understand that your management costs may have risen, but you must understand that my cost of living has also increased for the same reason—inflation.

Secondly, my copy of the lease shows that you agreed to perform certain maintenance services during my tenancy, yet in fact you have not carried them out. My apartment is overdue for (**painting/specific repairs/new carpet/drapes/appliance, etc.**). Although I have repeatedly requested this maintenance, you have yet to contact me to even arrange a time.

Until this service is performed, I will remain steadfastly against any increase. If need be, I will petition other tenants on their positions and organize a formal group protest.

In the interest of fairness, I respectfully request that you reconsider this increase until the above concerns have been resolved.

Sincerely,

Requesting Property Repairs

Dear (**name of landlord/property manager**):

I am writing to request repair service on the (**stove/refrigerator/sink, etc.**) in my apartment, which is unit number (**number**) of (**address**). The problem is that the (**stove/refrigerator/sink, etc.**) is (**describe problem**).

Please send a maintenance worker to repair it as soon as possible, as the problem is causing a major inconvenience. The best time to come would be (**day**), from (**time**) to (**time**). If that is unsuitable, please contact me at (**telephone number**) so that we may arrange an agreeable time.

Thank you for your prompt attention to this matter.

Sincerely,

Security Deposit Refund Request

Dear (**name of landlord/property manager**):

As you know, on (**date**), I vacated apartment number (**number**) at (**address**). As you may also be aware, according to the terms of my rental agreement, I was entitled to a refund of my security deposit no later than (**date**). The conditions of this agreement were that my record of payment should be in good standing and that the apartment did not require major cleaning or repairs.

I believe I have met all those conditions. However, as of this date, I have yet to receive the refund nor have I been given an explanation for the delay. In fact, I have even been frustrated in my attempts to contact the manager.

Please contact (**name of apartment manager**) immediately and insist that (**he/she**) send this refund right away, to the following address:

(**Your name and address**)

If you need to contact me for any reason, I can be reached at (**telephone number**).

Thank you for your prompt attention to this matter.

Sincerely,

Advising Tenant of Responsibility for Guests

Dear (**name of tenant**):

I appreciate you notifying me of the unfortunate incident that occurred on (**date**). As I understand it, one of your guests (**describe damage incurred**).

You will find that your lease clearly states that in fact you are responsible for any property damage incurred by your house guests; therefore, I cannot agree to pay for the cost of (**repairing/replacing**) the damaged items.

I suggest you urge your guest to pay for the damages. If that proves unsuccessful, you must pay for them yourself.

I am sorry for your misfortune, but I am afraid that I must enforce this rule and hold you responsible for resolving the problem.

Thank you for your cooperation.

Sincerely,

Notice of Late Rent Payments

Dear (**name of tenant**):

I have noticed that for the past (**number**) months, your rent payment has been at least (**number**) days late. Additionally, (**number**) more times your rent payment was received during the (**number of days**)-day grace period.

If you expect this to be a recurring problem, then I must insist that we discuss this matter immediately. If not, then I will expect your rent on the (**first/fifteenth, etc.**) day of each month from here on, as we agreed in the lease. I will overlook this problem if it is only temporary, but I must be aware of any more serious problems if it is not. If I do not hear from you within one week from the above date, I will assume your payments will heretofore be submitted on time.

Thank you for your cooperation.

Sincerely,

Notice of New Landlord

Dear (**name of tenant**):

This is to hereby notify you that I have sold the (**house/ apartment building/etc.**) you are currently residing in at (**address**) to (**name of new owner**). Please make your next rent check payable to (**name**) and send it to (**address**) by (**date**).

I have enjoyed our association in the past, and I have assured the new owner that you are an excellent tenant. I wish you the best for the future.

Thank you for your cooperation.

Sincerely,

Notice of Rent Increase

Dear (**name of tenant**):

This is to hereby notify you of my intent to increase your monthly rent from (**amount**) to (**amount**), effective (**date**). I regret that this has become necessary due to increases in the cost of maintaining the property.

Should you have any questions or concerns, please call me at (**telephone number**).

Thank you for your cooperation.

Sincerely,

Warning to Problem Tenants

Dear (**name of tenant**):

It has come to my attention that several residents in your building at (**address**) are experiencing frustration over your (**describe offending behavior**). They have urged me to correct the situation.

I respect your right to privacy in your apartment; however, you in turn must understand that you are living in a communal building, wherein it is easy to disturb your neighbors. You must therefore respect their right to peace.

Since your behavior has become disruptive to other tenants, I must insist that you stop (**type of offending behavior**) immediately, or risk eviction. If you do not alter your behavior, I will have no choice but to serve you with an eviction notice and/or contact the police.

In short, just be considerate of your neighbors and correct your behavior accordingly. Thank you for your cooperation.

Sincerely,

SIXTEEN

Insurance

Ah, insurance—the black hole of finance. It is interesting that an idea that would appear on paper to be so voluntary has become so universally accepted as necessary in our culture.

It's a simple concept: many people throw money into a pot so that if one of them needs it for an emergency, it's there. Yet, since no one can really predict the future or truly understand the statistics and probabilities of accidents, we simply give in to the idea that we must have this protection.

As a result, insurance companies are now among the richest and most powerful conglomerates in the western world. And they do make mistakes. So it's your job to watch your own account, to call them on an error, and to shop around for the best package deal.

In each of these cases, a smart letter is a powerful tool. It serves as both a cogent statement of purpose and a record, allowing you to enclose copies of documents that support your position. Take advantage of it!

Changing Your Beneficiary

Dear (**name of insurance agent**):

As of (**date**), I would like to change (**the/some of the**) (**beneficiary/beneficiaries**) on my life insurance policy. My policy number is (**number**).

Presently, (**name(s)**) (**is/are**) listed as my (**beneficiary/ beneficiaries**). I would like (**him/her/them**) to be replaced with (**name(s) of new beneficiary/beneficiaries**). All of the other information, such as amount and disbursement instructions, should remain unchanged.

Thank you for your assistance.

Sincerely,

Claiming Benefits: Auto Insurance

Dear (**name of claims representative**):

My policy number is (**number**). On (**date**), I reported to you the occurrence of an accident which damaged my vehicle, a (**year, make, and model of car**), license number (**number**). The car was (**describe damage**). After filling out the necessary forms and complying with your claims adjuster, (**name**), I was told I would be receiving a settlement check for (**amount**) to cover the cost of the (**damage/loss**).

I have not yet received that check. If you have already sent it, please disregard this letter. If not, please contact me immediately to explain the reason for the delay and inform me as to when I can expect to receive it. As you can understand, I am eager to be compensated for my (**damage/loss**) as quickly as possible, since it is a major inconvenience to be (**driving an unsafe car/without a car**), and I cannot (**repair/replace**) my vehicle without your settlement.

If you have any questions, please call me at (**telephone number**). Thank you for your prompt attention to this matter.

Sincerely,

Claiming Benefits: Homeowner's Insurance

Dear (**name of claims representative**):

On (**date**), my home, located at (**address**) in (**name of city**), was severely damaged by (**describe occurrence**). As a policyholder in good standing, I am therefore requesting a settlement of my policy, (**policy number**), in the amount of (**amount**), according to the terms in the contract.

I appreciate your prompt attention to this matter, since this (**damage/loss**) has seriously disrupted the lives of myself and my family. If you have any questions, or require any further information, please contact me at the above address or at (**telephone number**).

Thank you for your cooperation.

Sincerely,

Claiming Benefits: Life Insurance

Dear **(name of claims representative)**:

Please find enclosed a Certificate of Death, which I am submitting to notify you of the passing of your policyholder, **(name)**. It will show that **(he/she)** died on **(date)** in **(location)**.

I am the beneficiary of **(his/her)** life insurance policy, and as such I am therefore requesting a settlement of the policy, **(policy number)**, in the amount of **(amount)**, according to the terms in the contract.

If you require any additional information or have any questions, please contact me at the above address or at **(telephone number)**.

Thank you for your prompt attention to this matter.

Sincerely,

Inquiring to Insurance Commissioner About a Company

Dear **(name of state insurance commissioner, consumer division)**:

On **(date)**, I received a **(brochure/advertisement/ letter/ call from a salesperson)** from **(name of insurance company)**, offering me an interesting deal on **(auto/ health/life, etc.)** coverage. Specifically, they offered **(describe coverage)** for **(length of time)**, at a cost of **(amount)**.

As tempting as this is, I am hesitant to respond because I am unfamiliar with the company, so I am requesting information on them so that I can make an informed decision.

Please, if you would, respond with the answers to the following questions: Is (**name of company**) currently licensed to operate in (**name of state**)? Do you have any evaluation of their past record on servicing claims? Have there been any complaints, and if so, of what nature? What is their financial base? Their overall rating?

Thank you for assistance in providing the answers to any or all of my inquiries.

Sincerely,

Notification to Insurance Company of Policy Cancellation

Dear (**name of insurance company customer service representative/agent/broker**):

This letter is to hereby notify you of my intent to cancel my (**health/life/auto/fire, etc.**) policy with (**name of insurance company**), effective (**date**).

Since signing the policy agreement on (**date**), I have reevaluated my coverage, and decided that it is not sufficient for my needs. Specifically, I have found that (**the rates are too high/other customers have expressed concern about your ability to process settle-**

ments fairly, etc.), and I believe I can find more suitable terms elsewhere.

The amount of (**amount**) that I paid on (**date**) covers (**length of time**), so I request that you pro-rate the unused portion of my policy and refund the amount to me to the address above.

Thank you for your prompt attention to this matter.

Sincerely,

Response to Increase in Premium

Dear (**name of insurance company customer service representative/agent/broker**):

Recently, I was notified of your intention to increase the annual premium on my (**type of insurance**) policy from (**amount**) to (**amount**). I must respectfully protest this increase, based on the following:

First, I understand that your management costs may have risen, but you must understand that my cost of living has also increased for the same reason—inflation.

Secondly, I have been less than satisfied with the service I have received from your company. When I attempted to (**inquire/complain/file a claim**) on (**date**), I was (**describe complaint**). It is unreasonable to increase the cost of a service that is already less than exemplary.

Thirdly, I have inquired about rates on similar coverage from other companies, and have been informed that I can receive comparable—and in some cases lower—rates from a few of these companies. However, I would just as soon keep the matter simple and resolve my differences with your company. I merely request that you hold my rate at its current level, and provide more efficient and pleasant service.

Thank you in advance for your prompt attention to this matter.

Sincerely,

Response to Insurance Company's Termination of Policy

Dear (**name of state insurance commissioner, consumer division**):

On (**date**), I received a letter notifying me that (**name of insurance company**) was canceling my (**type of policy**) insurance policy, effective immediately. I have carried (**type of insurance**) insurance with this company for (**length of time**), and to my knowledge there is no justifiable reason for this cancellation.

I was a policyholder in good standing, having always paid my premiums on time. As for claims, (**describe history of claims**). This, in my judgment, is not sufficient reason for cancellation, especially considering my history with the company and the total amount of (**amount**) I have paid in premiums over (**length of time**).

Until now, I have been satisfied with this company, and would prefer to remain a policyholder with them. Not only is it inconvenient to search elsewhere, but securing coverage with a new company may prove more difficult in light of this cancellation.

I would appreciate it if you could look into the reasons behind this cancellation, and if possible, convince the company to reconsider their action.

Thank you very much for your assistance in this matter.

Sincerely,

Unacceptable Settlement of a Lost/Damaged Item

Dear (**name of claims representative**):

I am writing to express my disagreement with the amount of (**amount**) that your company has agreed to remit to settle the (**damage/loss**) of my (**type of item**), pursuant to your notification of (**date**), regarding my (**type of policy**) insurance policy, (**policy number**).

I believe you have overlooked the fact that this item appreciates in value over time. Your amount is based on its original (**cost**). I have enclosed a (**type of document**), which appraises a similar item at a higher value than its original cost. Therefore, I am requesting that you remit the amount of (**amount**) to cover the item's actual value at the time of its (**damage/loss**).

Thank you for your cooperation in this matter.

Sincerely,

SEVENTEEN

Medical Concerns

Nothing is more important than good health. This fact becomes especially obvious in times of illness or injury.

Consequently, quality health care is of utmost importance. And as the cost of good health care continually rises, spawning other issues, complications, and a sense of powerlessness, you can help maintain a sense of personal control by writing an effective letter.

A good letter can dispute an error on a bill, help you find out more information about a disease, and even authorize a friend or relative to make a potentially life-saving decision in the event of your inability to do so. That's power.

Appreciation of Care

Dear (**name of physician/nurse/administrator**):

I would like to express my appreciation for the fine care you gave me while I was undergoing treatment for (**type of condition**) at (**name of facility**).

I especially appreciated your honesty about my situation. Although it is not easy to accept bad news, you do far more service by communicating the facts honestly than if you were to pleasantly avoid the real issues.

So thank you for the excellent care—my health greatly improved because of your efforts—and generous attention to my needs. I will be sure to recommend you to friends and associates in the future.

Sincerely,

Arranging for Monthly Payments

Dear (**name of office manager**):

I recently received a statement which shows that I owe Dr. (**name of doctor**) a total of (**amount**). Unfortunately, my current finances do not allow me to pay the full amount by the date indicated.

Would it be possible to arrange monthly payments? I would make such payments regularly until the balance is all cleared up.

At the time, I feel that I can afford a monthly payment

of (**amount**). This would mean that the balance would be paid in full by (**date**).

Please let me know if this is satisfactory to you. I will be looking forward to your response. Thank you.

Sincerely,

Authorization to Release Medical Records

Dear Dr. (**name of your doctor**):

I hereby authorize you to release my medical file to (**name of doctor/insurance company/etc.**). (**He/she/they**) requested to see my file in order to (**specify reason(s)**). My insurance policy specifies that, in certain instances, a second opinion must be obtained before they will agree to cover the costs of treatment.

I would appreciate it if you could act on this matter as soon as possible.

Sincerely,

Disputed Bill

Dear (**name of office manager**):

On (**date**) I came in to see Dr. (**name of doctor**). During that visit, (**describe treatment/procedure that was performed**).

According to a statement I recently received from your office, I am being charged for the following: (**describe procedure or medication you are being billed for**). This is incorrect, as (**this procedure was not performed/I was not given this medication**).

Please make the necessary corrections and send me a new and revised statement. Thank you.

Sincerely,

Disputing Denial of Insurance

Dear (**name of doctor/office manager**):

On (**date**), I was told that your office now has a policy of not filing insurance claims. I believe this an unrealistic, even outrageous, position to take, in light of the fact that most of your patients cannot afford your care otherwise.

By insisting that payment be made in full upon treatment, you force your patients into a situation of financial hardship, as we must then file the claims ourselves and wait for months to be reimbursed. This makes us think twice about even agreeing to treatment, thus possibly endangering our health.

I urge you to reconsider this policy, for the health of your patients.

Sincerely,

Emergency Authorization of Medical Care

Attention: **(name of doctor/facility administrator)**

I, **(your name)**, hereby authorize my **(husband/wife/son/daughter/etc.)**, **(name)**, of **(address)**, to **(secure and/or authorize)** any appropriate and/or necessary medical care in the event that I am unable to do so, for myself or for my **(husband/wife/son/daughter/etc.)** This authorization applies only to emergency medical care, and is valid from **(date)** to **(date)**.

(Note: sign and date this form, then have it notarized and distributed to any appropriate parties (physician, appointee, ambulance service, hospital administrator), and keep one copy for yourself.)

Ending Medical Treatment

Dear **(name of doctor/facility administrator)**:

(I/my relative), **(your name/name of relative)**, **(have/has)** been receiving **(type of treatment)** from you since **(date)**. However, in the past **(length of time)**, **(my/his/her)** condition has grown steadily worse, and now I have become quite alarmed at **(my/his/her)** current state of health.

Meanwhile, my attempts to discuss this situation with you have been less than satisfying. In fact, I am shocked by your lack of concern for **(my/his/her)** condition, given the amount of money **(I/we)** have spent on this treatment. As a result, you have left **(me/us)** with no choice but to discontinue this treatment, effective **(date)**, and seek more attentive care elsewhere.

Please forward a copy of **(my/name of patient's)** medical records under your care to **(name and address of new physician or facility)**. Thank you for your cooperation.

Sincerely,

Researching Information About a Disease

Dear **(name of information officer of health organization)**:

I am seeking information about **(type of disease)**, a condition with which **(I/my relative)**, **(your name/name of relative)**, **(have/has)** been recently diagnosed. Under the circumstances, I would like to learn as much as possible about this disease. What options are available for its treatment, and what are their success rates? What are all of the symptoms and dangers of **(type of disease)**? What is its history?

I understand that your organization provides interested parties with **(brochures/information packets/other materials)** to help victims understand and cope with its difficulties, and offers services to help deal effectively with it.

Please send any appropriate information to the address above, and any additional information you feel may be appropriate.

Thank you very much for your assistance and prompt attention.

Sincerely,

EIGHTEEN

Military Affairs

If you're a veteran, you have no doubt discovered that the Department of Veterans Affairs is mired in endless bureaucracy. While the benefits eventually outweigh the negatives, this mountain of red tape does present a serious challenge to getting what you want or need. A good letter addressed to the right person will cut right through that red tape.

The same can be said for the branches of the U.S. Military. We've all heard about those obscene spending practices, like paying $600 for a pencil. Avoid getting caught in a voice-mail loop and write a letter!

Applying for a VA Home Loan

Dear (**name of Veterans Affairs officer**):

As a veteran of (**name of branch of service**), I am interested in obtaining a home loan through my GI benefits. Please send me a copy of form (**number**), Request for Determination of Eligibility and Available Loan Guaranty Entitlement. This is the first time I have applied for a VA home loan.

I served in the (**name of branch of service**) from (**date**) to (**date**), and was honorably discharged on (**date**) as a (**rank**). This means that I served more than the required 181 days, enabling me to qualify for this benefit. My (**service/Social Security**) number is (**number**).

I would greatly appreciate it if you could forward the form to the address above. Thank you for your cooperation.

Sincerely,

Changing Discharge Status

Dear (**name of member of the Review Board**):

I am writing to you to request a review of my (**classification of discharge**) discharge from (**name of branch of service**), which occurred on (**date**). I believe there is sufficient information to support such a review, as well as a reclassification of the discharge itself.

(Describe circumstances which were inaccurate/ under-represented at time of original discharge.)

I have enclosed the Department of Defense form (**number**) for this purpose. If you require any additional information, or if you have any questions regarding this matter, please contact me at the address on the form or at (**telephone number**).

Thank you for your consideration.

Sincerely,

Claiming Benefits: Service Life Insurance

Dear (**name of Veterans Affairs officer**):

Please find enclosed a Certificate of Death, issued by (**name of official and organization**), which I am submitting to notify you of the passing of (**name**). It will show that (**he/she**) died on (**date**) in (**name of city**), (**name of state**).

I am the beneficiary of (**his/her**) National Service Life Insurance policy, and as such I am requesting payment of the policy's settlement amount of (**amount**), as stated in the policy (**policy number**).

If you require any additional information or have any questions, please contact me at the above address or at (**telephone number**).

Thank you for your prompt attention to this matter.

Sincerely,

Disputing Denial of VA Benefits

Dear (**name of Veterans Affairs officer**):

On (**date**), I submitted a claim for (**type of VA benefits**), a copy of which I have enclosed. Then, on (**date**), I received notification from your office that this claim has been denied.

I believe this claim is valid, for several reasons. (**Describe circumstances/your position.**) Therefore, I am requesting both a disclosure of the reasons for its denial from the Department of Veterans Affairs office and an appellate review of this case. My (**service/ Social Security number**) is (**number**).

Please forward this letter to the appropriate department or individual responsible for conducting this review. If you require any additional information or if you have any questions, please contact me at the address above or at (**telephone number**).

Thank you for your cooperation.

Sincerely,

Request for MIA Information

Dear (**name of Veterans Affairs officer**):

On (**date**), my (**father/son/brother, etc.**), (**rank**), (**full name**), was declared missing in action while serving with (**name of unit**) of (**name of branch of service**) in (**name of location**). I am interested in contacting anyone who served with him during his period in the service or in that particular unit. His (**service/Social Security**) number was (**number**).

I would greatly appreciate any contact information you can provide me, as well as information on reunions or activities for this group. You may contact me at the above address or at (**telephone number**).

Thank you for your cooperation.

Sincerely,

Requesting a Copy of Military Document

Dear (**name of personnel records officer**):

I would like to obtain a copy of (**type of document**) that was issued on (**date**), since I seem to have misplaced my original copy.

My full name is (**your full name (with maiden name if applicable**)) and my (**service/Social Security**) number is (**number**). I served in the (**name of branch of service**) from (**date**) to (**date**).

This document is necessary for me to (**describe reason(s)—i.e., obtain employment/obtain education benefits, etc.**), so it is important that I possess a copy. Thank you very much for your prompt assistance.

Sincerely,

Requesting Federal Employment

Dear **(name of Veterans Affairs officer)**:

I am interested in obtaining information about employment opportunities within the federal government in **(name of location where you currently reside)**.

As a **(veteran/relative of a veteran)** of **(name of branch of service)**, I am aware that I may be able to obtain federal employment through the Vietnam Veterans Readjustment Assistance Act of 1974. **(I/my relative)** served in **(name of branch of service)** during the Vietnam War from **(date)** to **(date)**. **(My/his/her) (service/Social Security)** number is **(number)**.

Please forward any information you may have about federal employment to the address above. Thank you very much.

Sincerely,

NINETEEN

Press and Media

Just as there is much frustration with government these days, there is just as much frustration and mistrust of the media. But you need not feel so helpless. Write! You'll be surprised at what kinds of changes you can instigate by a timely, well-written letter.

The following samples will help you communicate your opinions to those in charge of television and radio stations, newspapers, and magazines. We'll also look at what to write when you find an advertisement to be particularly offensive.

Complaining About Television Program Content

Dear (**name of network executive**):

As I was viewing "(**name of program**)" on (**date**), I was shocked by the nature of its portrayal of (**describe offensive content**). I also found it disturbing that this program was aired in the early evening hours, when it is easily viewed by children. Not only is it deplorable to air a program with this type of content, it is downright irresponsible to air it so early.

I urge you to either cancel the program, tone down its subject matter to where it is appropriate for family viewing, or at the very least, air it at an hour when children are not awake to see it.

Thank you for your consideration.

Sincerely,

Consumer Action Reporter Request

Dear (**name of consumer action reporter**):

As a longtime fan of your segment on the channel (**number**) news program, I believe you may be able to help me resolve a frustrating situation, or at least, expose its true nature so that your viewers may benefit from my experience.

(**Describe your problem in detail, from its starting point to its current state, including the steps you have**

taken to resolve it. Enclose copies of any material which supports your case. Make it clear that you are now at a point where the intervention of such a reporter could make a clear difference, both to you and the general public.)

I urge you to investigate this situation further so that we may not only solve my problem, but help ensure that it does not happen to others. Of course, I am happy to provide whatever assistance you may need. You may contact me at (**telephone number**).

Thank you for your consideration.

Sincerely,

Editorial Opinion Against an Issue

Dear (**name of station general manager or editor**):

I am writing to express my disagreement with your position on (**type of issue**), of which your (**station manager/newspaper writer**) (**spoke/wrote**) recently.

(**Describe your specific stance on the issue, and why you feel the published/aired position is wrong.**)

I applaud your decision to take a stand on this issue; however, I believe that it is (**misinformed/detrimental to the long-term public interest, etc.**) I know that many other citizens in this community feel the same way as I do, including (**names of prominent citizens**). In the interest of balanced public debate, I request that you (**publish/air**) this or a similar opposing viewpoint.

Thank you very much for your consideration.

Sincerely,

Editorial Opinion In Favor of an Issue

Dear (**name of editor or station general manager**):

I am writing to express my agreement with your position on (**type of issue**), which your (**station manager/ newspaper writer**) voiced so eloquently recently.

(**Describe your specific stance on the issue.**)

I applaud your decision to take a stand on this issue, and fully support your position. I believe that by doing so, you have provoked further thought on the issue on the part of your (**viewers/readers**), and that can only be healthy.

Sincerely,

Newspaper Classified Ad

Dear (**name of advertising representative**):

Please place the following classified advertisement in your (**date(s)**) edition, under the (**type of section—i.e., autos/office equipment, etc.**) heading.

(Type classified ad exactly as you want it to read, and double-check it for mistakes.)

I have enclosed a check for (**amount**), made out to (**name of publication**). I understand the ad will run for (**number**) days for this price. If you have any questions, please call me at (**telephone number**).

Thank you for your assistance.

Sincerely,

Protesting Cancellation of a Show

Dear (**name of network executive**):

I recently read that your network has decided to cancel "(**name of program**)." This news was particularly disturbing to (**me/my family**), since (**I/we**) watch this show religiously and always thoroughly enjoy it.

I understand that your decisions are based primarily on ratings, and that the reason you canceled "(**name of program**)" was because its ratings were not sufficiently high to attract sponsors for it. At the same time, I would hope that if enough loyal fans expressed their support for the show, we could save it.

To that end, I have encouraged all those I know to write or call your office. I also have a suggestion: Why not try a different time slot, one that is perhaps more conducive to attracting the show's target viewers, and one that is a little less competitive? I am sure you have considered this option, but would it hurt to try it?

We need more shows like "(**name of program**)," not less of them. I urge you to reconsider this decision.

Sincerely,

Request for Airing a Public Service Announcement

Dear (**name of station program director**):

On (**date**), the (**name of charity/non-profit organization**) will be holding a (**type of event**) at (**name of location**) from (**date**) to (**date**). This event will raise money for (**name of charity**), and is open to the public. The (**type of event**) is of interest to the public because it will (**describe the ways its fundraising may help the public**).

(**Name of organization**) would greatly appreciate it if you would broadcast this information on your station (**at/during**) (**time/"name of program"**).

I have enclosed the appropriate promotional and background materials. If you need any additional information, please contact me at (**telephone number**).

Thank you for your assistance.

Sincerely,

TWENTY

Products

With the proliferation of home shopping networks, infomercials, and various other mail-order services, more of us are shopping from home than ever before. And with the "Information Superhighway," it appears this trend will only increase.

As such, the chances that a company will make a mistake on your purchase are high and getting higher. What's more, there are other situations that may not involve an error by a retailer, but where you still may need to write a letter. Maybe you've discovered that a product you purchased is missing a part, or that your favorite store does not stock a product you would like to purchase. Whatever the reason, a letter lets the retailer or manufacturer know, in no uncertain terms, what you desire.

Claiming a Repair for a Product Under Warranty

Dear (**name of customer service representative**):

Enclosed please find a (**type of product**), which I purchased on (**date**). I understand that your company provides a warranty for this product for (**length of time**), and I am requesting that you repair it under the provisions of this warranty.

You will find that the product shows no signs of mistreatment, nor have I attempted to repair it myself. If the product cannot be repaired, please replace it, or credit me with its value.

I have also enclosed a copy of the store receipt, as well as a copy of the warranty and sufficient postage to return the item after you are finished repairing it.

Thank you for your cooperation.

Sincerely,

Damaged/Defective Item

Dear (**name of customer service representative**):

On (**date**) I ordered a (**type of product**) from your company. I received the product today, and was extremely disappointed to find that it was (**damaged/ defective**). (**Describe the damage/defection.**)

In accordance with your guarantee, I am returning the item. I look forward to receiving a replacement (**type of product**) within (**number**) (**days/weeks**).

Thank you for your prompt attention.

Sincerely,

Misrepresentation

Dear (**name of customer service representative**):

On (**date**) I ordered a (**type of product**) from your company. I received the product today, and was extremely disappointed when I opened the package. The (**type of product**) is (**describe problem**). It certainly does not live up to the expectations I had (and you raised) when I first saw it in your (**advertisement/catalog**).

Because I do not feel that you represented the product in a fair manner, and since I believe the price I paid is too much for an item of this quality, I am returning the (**type of product**). I trust that a refund in the amount of (**amount**) will be sent to me expeditiously.

Thank you for your prompt attention.

Sincerely,

Ordering a Product by Mail

Dear (**name of customer service representative**):

Please send me the following item from your catalog: Item number (**number**), listed on page (**number**) of your catalog, in size (**size**), (**color**). I have enclosed a check in the amount of **(amount)** to cover the cost of this item and the shipping charges.

Should there be any problems with this order, please return my check and cancel my order—I do not want substitutions.

Thank you for processing this order quickly. I look forward to receiving it within **(length of time specified in catalog/advertisement)**.

Sincerely,

Potentially Dangerous Toy

Dear **(name of product safety manager)**:

On **(date)**, I purchased your product, a **(brand name and type of product)**, then gave it to my **(son/daughter/etc.)**. To my alarm, **(describe what happened, and how the product aroused your fears)**.

As a result, I do not believe you should be selling this product to minors, as it presents a serious risk to children. Indeed, it was fortunate for both of us that nothing more serious happened to my **(son/daughter, etc.)**.

I urge you to **(correct the problem/recall this product)**, so that this potential danger is removed from the shelves.

Sincerely,

Product Never Delivered

Dear (**name of customer service representative**):

I would like to call to your attention a service discrepancy.

On (**date**), I ordered a (**type of product**) from your company. I also (**enclosed a check/charged my credit card account**) for (**amount**). It was my understanding that I would receive the (**type of product**) within (**length of time**).

It is now (**date**), and I have not received the (**type of product**). But my records show that you (**canceled my check/charged my account**) on (**date**), and I have enclosed a copy of the (**canceled check/credit statement**) as proof.

If the product has not yet been sent, please deliver it immediately. If there is a problem, please contact me immediately to explain the reason for the delay. I understand that sometimes unforeseen problems occur, but I find it irresponsible not to notify customers of delays.

Thank you for your prompt attention to this matter.

Sincerely,

Received the Wrong Item

Dear (**name of customer service representative**):

On (**date**), I ordered a (**type of item**) from you. However, I recently received a package from you containing a (**type of item**), which I did not order—nor did I receive the item I indeed ordered.

Therefore, I am returning this item, and I am requesting that you send out my original order urgently. If there is a problem, please contact me immediately at (**telephone number**) to explain.

Thank you for your cooperation.

Sincerely,

TWENTY ONE

Schools

Our education system is changing rapidly. Parents, teachers and school administrators are trying to maintain old-fashioned standards while at the same time attempting to keep up with modern technology and a variety of problems, such as overcrowded classrooms, non-English-speaking students, and even increasing violence.

Yet many universals still apply. The following sample letters should comprise the most common—and even traditional—examples of messages.

Appreciation of Teacher

Dear (**name of principal**):

I am writing to you to express my appreciation of my (**son/daughter**)'s teacher, (**name of teacher**). Under (**his/her**) supervision, my (**son/daughter**) has shown remarkable improvement on several levels: (**his/her**) grades are improving, (**he/she**) is doing (**his/her**) homework more often, and (**he/she**) seems genuinely excited about going to school.

Moreover, my conversations with (**name of teacher**) have always been pleasant and informative. I am impressed with the respect and admiration my child has shown for (**him/her**), and having met with (**him/her**) on occasion, I can see why.

You should be very proud to have (**name of teacher**) on your staff, and I felt that you should be aware of the excellent work (**he/she**) is doing. (**He/she**) deserves any commendation or promotion you may be able to give (**him/her**).

Sincerely,

Disputing a Grade

Dear (**name of dean of students/department head**):

I am writing to dispute the grade of (**grade**) I was awarded in (**name of course**), taught by (**name of instructor**). I believe it is incorrect, for the following reasons.

(**Name of instructor**) clearly informed the class that grades were awarded according to a point system. However, while I have earned (**number**) points, which is more than the necessary number to qualify for (**a/an**) (**grade**), in fact I was awarded a grade of (**grade**).

In the highly competitive academic world, little differences could mean a lot; therefore, I feel justified in insisting that my grade be changed from (**a/an**) (**grade**) to (**a/an**) (**grade**).

Please take the necessary action to make this change. I appreciate your help in resolving this matter. If you have any questions, please contact me at (**telephone number**).

Thank you for your cooperation.

Respectfully,

Excusing a Child from Physical Education

Dear (**name of teacher**):

I am writing to request that you excuse my (**son/daughter/etc.**) from your physical education class. (**He/she**) suffers from (**describe limitation**), and therefore will be unable to perform the necessary physical exertion for this class.

I have enclosed a statement from (**name of student's doctor**) as supporting evidence.

I also ask that you assign (**name of student**) to an alternate class or a special assignment that will allow (**him/her**) to fulfill (**his/her**) school requirements to pass this class.

If you need any additional information, or if I can answer any questions, please contact me at (**telephone number**).

Thank you for your cooperation.

Sincerely,

Reinstatement Request

Dear (**name of dean of admissions**):

I was formerly a student at (**name of school**) from (**date**) to (**date**), but found it necessary to withdraw due to (**describe reason(s)**). However, I have resolved (**this/those**) (**problem/problems**), and would now like to be reinstated to (**name of school**), beginning with the (**spring/fall/etc.**) (**semester/term**).

You will find my original application and transcript under my full name, (**full name**), and student number, (**number**). If you require me to fill out any new forms, I will be happy to do so. If you require any other information or an interview, I will be available to meet with you at your convenience. You may contact me at the address above or at (**telephone number**).

Thank you for your cooperation.

Sincerely,

Requesting Information on Admission and Financial Aid

Dear **(name of registrar)**:

(I/my son/daughter/other) **(am/is)** considering furthering **(my/his/her)** education next **(fall/spring/etc.)** term, and to that end, I am exploring various educational options. **(I/we)** **(am/are)** interested in your institution for **(describe reasons)**.

I would appreciate it if you would send **(me/us)** a copy of your current catalog and any pertinent admissions information at your earliest convenience. Also, if you could, please send additional information on financial aid opportunities and programs, including any available scholarships.

Thank you for your assistance.

Sincerely,

Requesting Transcript Copy

Dear **(name of registrar)**:

I am interested in obtaining **(number)** copies of my transcript, and to that end, I have enclosed a check for **(amount)** to cover the cost of this service. I have found that it is necessary to provide certain prospective employers with this information.

I was a student at (**name of school or college**) from (**month**), (**year**), to (**month**), (**year**), and I graduated with a (**degree/certificate**) in (**major**). My (**student i.d. number/Social Security number**) is (**number**).

Please send this information at your earliest convenience. Thank you for your assistance.

Sincerely,

Volunteering to Help a School

Dear (**name of principal**):

I would like to offer my services as a volunteer to your school. I am a resident of the area, I have some free time, and I can think of no better way to spend it than to support the education of future generations and give something back to my community. Plus, it would give me great joy to spend some time around children.

Specifically, I would be happy to help out in the (**library/administrative office/cafeteria/playground, etc.**). I have special skills in (**describe skills**), so that would be my first preference. I am available on (**days of week**), from (**time**) to (**time**).

Please contact me at your convenience so that we may discuss the details further. Thank you for your consideration.

Sincerely,

Withdrawing from School

Dear (**name of department head/dean of students**):

It comes with great regret that I must inform you of my intention to withdraw from school because of (**describe reason(s)**). Unfortunately, my current circumstances are such that I am left with no other options.

I have enjoyed and benefited from my enrollment here, and I appreciate all the help and valuable advice you have given me during (**length of time**). I hope that when the time comes for me to reapply to this or another institution, I can rely upon you for a favorable recommendation.

Thank you for your understanding.

Sincerely,

TWENTY TWO

Services

Services differ from products in that you are paying for something intangible. The most common circumstances in this category include complaining about a service, canceling a service, or praising someone who has performed a service for you. As usual, remember to be tactful, but firm. If you feel you've been wronged, stick to your guns and do not be satisfied until the problem has been corrected.

Cancel a Service

Dear **(name of owner/customer service representative)**:

On **(date)** I hired **(you/your company)** to **(describe service)**. In the beginning, I was quite happy with your service. However, in recent **(days/weeks/months)**, I have become less and less enchanted with your work. **(Describe the problem.)**

Because of this problem, I would like to discontinue the service as of **(today/date)**. I'm sorry we could not work this out. Please send me a final bill.

Sincerely,

Canceling Cable TV Service

Dear **(name of customer service representative)**:

Please cancel my subscription to **(name of cable television company)**, effective **(date)**. I **(have enclosed a check for amount to cover the balance due/will expect a refund of amount for the time not used)**.

Although cable television is a fine service, I can no longer justify the time to view it, nor the funds to pay for it. As my budget tightens, I find I must eliminate the non-essentials.

Thank you for your fine service and your prompt attention to this matter.

Sincerely,

Canceling a Subscription

Dear (**name of circulation manager**):

Please cancel my subscription to (**name of publication**), effective (**date**). I (**have enclosed a check for amount to cover the balance due/will expect a refund of amount for undelivered issues**).

Although (**name of publication**) is a fine publication, I no longer have the time to read it, and thus I can no longer justify paying for a subscription on my tight budget. I find it smarter to buy a copy at the newsstand as the need arises.

Thank you for your fine service and your prompt attention to this matter.

Sincerely,

Complaint About Service

Dear (**name of owner/customer service representative**):

On (**date**), one of your employees, (**employee's name**), came to my home to (**describe the service performed**). I found (**his/her**) work to be thoroughly unsatisfactory. (**Describe the problem.**)

Because of this situation, I am refusing to pay your company until the problem is remedied.

Thank you for your prompt attention.

Sincerely,

Requesting Information About a Service

Dear (**name of customer service representative**):

I am interested in receiving information about the services your company provides—particularly in the area of (**describe specific interest**).

Please send the appropriate materials, brochures, and order forms to the above address. Thank you for your assistance.

Sincerely,

Thank You for a Service

Dear (**name of customer service representative**):

I just wanted to express my appreciation for the excellent (**type of service**) service your company has provided me. (**Describe specific example of satisfactory service.**)

It is becoming all too rare these days to find a company that goes to such great lengths to satisfy its customers. I hope your success will show others that old-fashioned hard work and consideration for customers are values that are rewarded in our society.

Best of luck in the future.

Sincerely,

Transferring Phone Service to a New Location

Dear (**name of customer service representative**):

On (**date**), I will be moving out of my residence at (**address**), to my new residence at (**address**). At that time, I would like to disconnect my telephone service at my current address and establish a new line at my new residence.

My current telephone number is (**telephone number**). Please advise me of my new phone number as quickly as possible. I wish to keep the same services that I currently use, as well as my current long-distance carrier, (**name of company**).

I understand that there are charges involved for this process, so please itemize those on the first bill sent to my new address.

Thank you for your cooperation.

Sincerely,

TWENTY THREE

Tax Issues

The I.R.S. is a daunting organization, an arm of the U.S. Government that most people dread communicating with, much less contesting. Of course, it is this attitude of the people that merely compounds the problem of the I.R.S.'s power.

There is no reason not to stand up to them. Again, we live in a democracy, it is your right to do so. And since there is so much red tape to weed through, it is vital that your letter stand out from the pack. Follow these guidelines and you'll be amazed at what you can accomplish.

Letter Accompanying Payment of Back Taxes

Dear (**name of I.R.S. official**):

Enclosed please find my check for (**amount**) to cover the full amount of taxes I owed for the year (**year**). I trust that this clears me of any further financial obligation in this matter.

I have also enclosed the completed form (**type of form**) documenting this transaction. If you require any further materials or information, please feel free to contact me at (**telephone number**). My full name is (**your full name**), and my (**Social Security number/federal tax i.d. number**) is (**number**).

Thank you for your cooperation.

Sincerely,

Protesting Amount of Tax Refund

Dear (**name of I.R.S. official**):

I am writing to clarify a potential bookkeeping error regarding the amount of my refund on my (**year**) taxes. First of all, the name on the return in question is (**your full name**), and my (**Social Security number/ federal tax i.d. number**) is (**number**).

According to the (**1040/1040A/etc.**) form I submitted, I am due a refund of (**amount**) for (**year**). However, I have just received a check from you in the amount of (**amount**).

After rechecking my figures, the amount I originally calculated still seems correct. If I am mistaken, please let me know. If not, please send me the difference of (**amount**) to the address above.

Thank you for your assistance.

Sincerely,

Protesting Amount of Taxes Owed

Dear (**name of I.R.S. official**):

I am writing to clarify a potential error regarding the amount I owe on my (**year**) taxes. First, the name on the return in question is (**name**), and my (**Social Security number/federal tax i.d. number**) is (**number**).

According to the (**1040/1040A/etc.**) form I submitted, I must pay (**amount**) for (**year**). However, I have just received correspondence from you indicating that you believe I owe (**amount**). This is incorrect, as I will show.

After rechecking my figures, the amount I originally calculated still seems correct. I have attached copies of my (**W-4 form/other forms**) indicating that you failed to (**credit taxes already withheld/note the number of dependents I actually have**). I have also attached the bottom half of the form you sent, as you requested. Please make the necessary corrections and acknowledge this adjustment via mail.

Thank you for your assistance.

Sincerely,

Requesting an Extension

Dear (**name of I.R.S. official**):

It has become necessary for me to request an extension on filing my income tax return for the year (**year**). Please make the necessary adjustment on my records and send the appropriate forms and instructions to the following address:

(**Your address**)

Thank you for your cooperation.

Sincerely,

Response to an Audit Notice

Dear (**name of I.R.S. official**):

I have received your correspondence informing me that my federal tax return for (**year**) is being audited. My full name is (**your full name**), and my (**Social Security number/federal tax i.d. number**) is (**number**).

I have enclosed, per your request, the following items for your review:

(**List items requested by I.R.S.—i.e., receipts, forms, any other materials that support your position.**)

If you require any additional materials or information, please contact me at (**telephone number**).

Sincerely,

Voicing Disagreement with Proposed Tax Increase

Dear **(name of senator/representative/local official)**:

I am writing to express my disagreement with the proposed increase in **(sales tax/gasoline tax/other)**. **(Explain your position: State the reasons why you feel this would cause a negative effect on the citizens in your community, state, or country.)**

I believe there are better ways to balance the budget, and with a little creative thinking and hard-line budgeting, we should be able to make up the difference. **(Suggest alternative ideas to raising taxes.)**

Thank you for your time and consideration.

Sincerely,

TWENTY FOUR

Travel

Taking a vacation or business trip can be quite complicated, especially if it involves travel to a foreign country. Finding out the best sightseeing spots, the best accommodations, disputing a hotel bill ... there are a bundle of situations which can be made less complex with an appropriate letter.

So where do you turn? Travel agents, the office of tourism, and foreign embassies are always helpful—they want you to travel, to have a good time, and to spend your money there, so don't be afraid to ask them for help. And given the price of a long distance or international phone call, a letter is by far the most effective means of communicating. You will also find it helpful to write to hotels and other businesses for a variety of purposes.

Canceling a Reservation

Dear (**name of hotel/rental car representative**):

I regret to inform you that I must cancel my reservation of a (**hotel room/rental car**) for (**date**) to (**date**), made under the name (**your name**). Unfortunately, (**describe reason for cancellation**). My confirmation number is (**number**).

Please credit my (**type of credit card**), (**credit card number**), which I used to guarantee the reservation on (**date**), and forward a written confirmation of this cancellation and credit to my attention at the address above or fax me at (**fax number**).

Thank you for your cooperation.

Sincerely,

Changing Information on Passport

Dear (**name of regional passport representative**):

I wish to amend the information on my passport, which was originally issued in (**month**), (**year**), to reflect my current name. I recently (**married/divorced/other**), and my legal name is now (**your full name**).

I have enclosed my passport, along with form (**number**) and a copy of (**legal document supporting name change, such as a marriage certificate**).

Please return the new passport and these documents to me at the above address.

Thank you.

Sincerely,

Complaint About Hotel Service

Dear (**name of hotel/motel official**):

I am writing to express my dissatisfaction for the manner in which my stay at your (**hotel/motel**) was handled.

I reserved a (**type of room**) on (**date**) at (**name of hotel/motel**) in (**name of city**), at (**address**). My reservation was for (**number**) days, from (**date**) to (**date**). I made these arrangements well in advance of my arrival, knowing that most of the local accommodations would fill up quickly, considering the popularity of the (**type of event**) the city was hosting. Shortly thereafter, I received the written confirmation in the mail of my reservation for a (**type of room**). I have attached a copy of this document.

However, when I arrived, I was told that in fact this type of room was not available, and I was assigned a (**type of room**) which featured none of my original preferences. Of course, at that late date, I was indeed unable to find my preferred accommodations elsewhere, and therefore had no choice but to accept the reservation under the circumstances.

I was given no acceptable reason for this mistake. Therefore, I believe I am justified in insisting that I be refunded (**part/all**) of the charges I incurred during my stay. I have also enclosed a copy of the final bill, and I hope to hear from you soon regarding this matter.

Thank you for your cooperation.

Sincerely,

Gaining Medical Clearance for a Cruise or Flight

Dear (**name of medical officer of cruise ship/airline**):

I am writing to request medical clearance for my (**spouse/child, etc.**), (**name of passenger**), on (**name of vessel/airline**), (**number**) to (**destination**) on (**date**).

To that end, I have enclosed a copy of a statement from (**name of passenger**)'s physician, (**name of doctor**), certifying that (**he/she**) is indeed able to undergo this travel. I will also provide additional information on medications and supporting medical data to the medical staff upon boarding.

If you have any questions or require any additional information, please contact me at (**telephone number**). Thank you for your cooperation and special attention.

Sincerely,

Inquiring About a Cruise

Dear (**name of cruise officer/travel agent**):

I am considering taking your (**name of cruise**)' to (**destination**) from (**date**) to (**date**). I would like to know what sort of packages you offer, including rooms, rates, amenities and discounts.

I prefer a (**size**) bed and (**describe any other preferences, such as a suite, room service, etc.**) What might you have available, and what are your rates, including possible discounts? What sort of meals and entertainment do you offer, and what are the ports of call?

Please send the answers to these questions and any other pertinent information or literature to my attention at the address above. Thank you for your assistance.

Sincerely,

Inquiring About a Hotel

Dear (**name of hotel manager**):

I am planning a trip to (**name of city in which hotel is located**) on (**date**), and would like to know what sort of rooms, rates, and amenities you offer.

I plan to stay in (**name of city**) for (**number**) nights, from (**date**) to (**date**). I prefer a (**size**) bed and (**describe any other preferences, such as an east view, a suite, room service, etc.**) What might you have available, and what are your rates? Also, please include any information on discounts you offer.

Thank you for your assistance.

Sincerely,

Inquiring About a Tour or Adventure Vacation

Dear (**name of travel agent/tour representative**):

I have heard that you offer a (**type of tour/adventure**) vacation, and I am interested in reading more about it.

What are the dates of your upcoming tours? How many people do you take on one trip? What are the backgrounds of the guides? What can I expect for accommodations? Are there any restrictions of which I should be aware? How much is the entire package, or do you have several different options? Do you offer any discounts?

Please send the answers to these questions and any other pertinent information or literature to my attention at the above address.

Thank you very much for your assistance.

Sincerely,

Making a Hotel or Rental Car Reservation

Dear **(name of hotel/rental car representative)**:

I would like to reserve a **(hotel room/rental car)** for **(date)** to **(date)** under the name of **(your name)**. My first preference is for **(type of room/beds/view or size of car/make/model, etc.)** **(If applicable:)** I have enclosed a **(coupon/type of document)** entitling me to a discount on this reservation.

As I am not certain of my arrival time on **(date)**, I would like to guarantee this reservation with my credit card, **(type of credit card)**, **(credit card number)**, expiration date **(month)** **(year)**.

Please confirm this reservation with an itemized projection of charges either by mailing it to the address above or faxing it to (**fax number**).

Thank you for your prompt attention.

Sincerely,

Requesting Information on International Health Restrictions

Dear (**name of U.S. Government Printing Office Superintendent of Documents**):

I am writing to request a copy of *Health Information for International Travel*, which I understand you provide for a cost of (**amount**). I have enclosed a check for that amount to cover the cost of sending this information.

In particular, I am interested in immunization requirements and information on what types of precautions I should take in my upcoming travels to the following countries: (**list countries**). If you can supply any additional information on restrictions in these areas, please include them as well. If there is an additional charge for this information, please let me know.

Thank you for your assistance.

Sincerely,

Requesting Tourist Information from U.S. Office of Tourism

Dear **(name of tourism officer)**:

(I/my family and I) **(am/are)** planning a visit to **(name of country)** in **(month)** of **(year)**. I understand that your office provides information to American tourists, and I am hoping your resources can help **(me/us)** better plan our trip.

Please provide me with any information pertinent to basic travel in **(name of country)**, such as customs, laws, travel restrictions, and health regulations. In addition, it would be very helpful if you could include brochures on travel tips, hotel rates, maps, and sight-seeing tours.

As this is **(my/our)** first visit to **(name of country)**, we are seeking all the help we can get, so virtually anything you deem pertinent would be greatly appreciated.

Thank you very much for your assistance.

Sincerely,

Requesting a Visa

Dear **(name of foreign country representative/embassy officer)**:

I am writing to request a **(business/student/personal/other)** visa for a visit to **(name of city/province/country)** in **(month)** of **(year)**. I intend to stay in (**location**) approximately (**length of time**).

I would like to know what materials you require from me in order to issue this visa. Also, assuming the visa is approved, will I be able to travel immediately thereafter, or must I wait for a period of time. If so, how long? And is there a fee required to enter or leave (**name of country**)?

Please send me any information that will answer these questions, as well as any additional information you regard as important, such as customs, health regulations, laws, and travel restrictions.

Thank you very much for your assistance.

Sincerely,

Thank You for Excellent Service

Dear (**name of hotel/motel manager**):

I am writing to express my appreciation for the excellent service (**I/my family and I**) received during (**my/our**) stay at your (**hotel/motel**).

(**Describe circumstances of arrival and stay, and cite examples of the staff performing over and above the norm.**)

Thank you for extending (**me/us**) such kindness and consideration. You can be sure that the next time (**I/we**) travel to your area, your fine establishment will be (**my/our**) first choice of accommodations.

Sincerely,

Appendix

Forms of Address

Government

PERSON	ADDRESS	SALUTATION
U.S. President	The President The White House Washington, DC 20500	Dear Mr. President
former President	The Honorable John Smith Address	Dear Mr. Smith
Vice President	The Vice President Executive Office Building Washington, DC 20501	Dear Mr. Vice President
Cabinet members	The Honorable John (or Jane) Smith The Secretary of **cabinet** or The Postmaster General or The Attorney General Washington, DC	Dear Mr. (or Madam) Secretary

PERSON	ADDRESS	SALUTATION
Chief Justice	The Chief Justice The Supreme Court Washington, DC 20543	Dear Mr. Justice (or Dear Mr. Chief Justice)
Associate Justice	Mr. Justice Smith or Madam Justice Smith The Supreme Court Washington, DC 20543	Dear Mr. (or Madam) Justice
U.S. Senator	The Honorable John (or Jane) Smith United States Senate Washington, DC 20001	Dear Senator Smith
Speaker of the House	The Honorable John (or Jane) Smith Speaker of the House of Representatives United States Capitol Washington, DC 20001	Dear Mr. (or Madam) Speaker

PERSON	ADDRESS	SALUTATION
U.S. Representative	The Honorable John (or Jane) Smith United States House of Representatives Washington, DC 20001	Dear Mr. (or Mrs., Ms.) Smith
U.N. Representative	The Honorable John (or Jane) Smith U.S. Representative to the United Nations United Nations Plaza New York, NY 10017	Dear Mr. (or Madam) Ambassador
Ambassador	The Honorable John (or Jane) Smith Ambassador of the United States American Embassy Address	Dear Mr. (or Madam) Ambassador

PERSON	ADDRESS	SALUTATION
Consul General	The Honorable John (or Jane) Smith American Consul General Address	Dear Mr. (or Mrs., Ms.) Smith
Foreign Ambassador	His (or Her) Excellency John (or Jane) Jones The Ambassador of **country** Address	Excellency or Dear Mr. (or Madam) Ambassador
Secretary-General of the U.N.	His (or Her) Excellency John (or Jane) Jones Secretary-General of the United Nations United Nations Plaza New York, NY 10017	Dear Mr. (or Madam) Secretary-General
Governor	The Honorable John (or Jane) Smith Governor of **state** State Capitol Address	Dear Governor Smith

PERSON	ADDRESS	SALUTATION
State legislators	The Honorable John (or Jane) Smith Address	Dear Mr. (or Mrs., Ms.) Smith
Judges	The Honorable John (or Jane) Smith Justice, Appellate Division Supreme Court of the State of **state** Address	Dear Judge Smith
Mayor	The Honorable John (or Jane) Smith His (or Her) Honor the Mayor City Hall Address	Dear Mayor Smith
City Council	The Honorable John (or Jane) Smith Councilman (or Councilwoman), City of **city** Address	Dear Mr. (or Mrs., Ms.) Smith

CLERGY

PERSON	ADDRESS	SALUTATION
The Pope	His Holiness, the Pope or His Holiness, Pope John Paul II Vatican City Rome, Italy	Your Holiness or Most Holy Father
Cardinals	His Eminence, John Cardinal Smith, Archbishop of **district** Address	Your Eminence or Dear Cardinal Smith
Bishops	The Most Reverend John Smith, Bishop (or Archbishop) of **district** Address	Your Excellency or Dear Bishop (Archbishop) Smith
Monsignor	The Right Reverend John Smith Monsignor Smith Address	Right Reverend Monsignor or Dear Monsignor Smith

PERSON	ADDRESS	SALUTATION
Priest	The Reverend John Smith Address	Reverend Father or Dear Father Smith
Brother	Brother John or Brother John Smith Address	Dear Brother John or Dear Brother
Sister	Sister Mary Jude Address	Dear Sister Mary Jude or Dear Sister
Protestant Clergy	The Reverend John Smith (or Jane Smith)	Dear Dr. (or Mr. or Ms.) Smith
Bishop (Episcopal)	The Right Reverend John Smith Bishop of district Address	Dear Bishop Smith
Rabbi	Rabbi Arthur (or Ruth) Simon Address	Dear Rabbi (or Dr.) Simon

MILITARY—Army, Air Force, Marines

PERSON	ADDRESS	SALUTATION
General of the Army	General John Smith U.S. Army (or Air Force or Marines) Address	Dear General Smith
Lieutenant General	General John Smith U.S. Army (or Air Force or Marines) Address	Dear General Smith
Brigadier General	General John Smith U.S. Army (or Air Force or Marines) Address	Dear General Smith
Lieutenant Colonel	Colonel John Smith U.S. Army (or Air Force or Marines) Address	Dear Colonel Smith
First Lieutenant	Lieutenant John Smith U.S. Army (or Air Force or Marines) Address	Dear Lieutenant Smith
Second Lieutenant All sergeants	Lieutenant John Smith U.S. Army (or Air Force or Marines) Address	Dear Lieutenant Smith

MILITARY—Navy, Coast Guard

PERSON	ADDRESS	SALUTATION
Fleet Admiral	Admiral John Smith U.S. Navy (or Coast Guard) Address	Dear Admiral Smith
Vice Admiral	Admiral John Smith U.S. Navy (or Coast Guard) Address	Dear Admiral Smith
Rear Admiral Lieutenant	Admiral John Smith U.S. Navy (or Coast Guard) Address	Dear Admiral Smith
Commander Lieutenant,	Commander John Smith U.S. Navy (or Coast Guard) Address	Dear Commander Smith
Junior Grade All chief petty officers	Lieutenant John Smith U.S. Navy (or Coast Guard) Address	Dear Lieutenant Smith

EDUCATION

PERSON	ADDRESS	SALUTATION
Dean of college or university	Dean John Smith name of college or university Address	Dear Dean Smith
President of college or university	Mr. John Smith, President name of college or university Address	Dear President Smith
President (with doctorate) of college or university	John Smith, Dr. of Law President, name of college or university Address	Dear Dr. Smith
Professor of college or university	Professor John Smith name of college or university Address	Dear Professor Smith
Professor (with doctorate) of college or university	Professor John Smith, Dr. of Law name of college or university Address	Dear Dr. Smith

JAICO PUBLISHING HOUSE

Elevate Your Life. Transform Your World.

ESTABLISHED IN 1946, Jaico Publishing House is home to world-transforming authors such as Sri Sri Paramahansa Yogananda, Osho, the Dalai Lama, Sri Sri Ravi Shankar, Sadhguru, Robin Sharma, Deepak Chopra, Jack Canfield, Eknath Easwaran, Devdutt Pattanaik, Khushwant Singh, John Maxwell, Brian Tracy, and Stephen Hawking.

Our late founder Mr. Jaman Shah first established Jaico as a book distribution company. Sensing that independence was around the corner, he aptly named his company Jaico ('Jai' means victory in Hindi). In order to service the significant demand for affordable books in a developing nation, Mr. Shah initiated Jaico's own publications. Jaico was India's first publisher of paperback books in the English language.

While self-help, religion and philosophy, mind/body/spirit, and business titles form the cornerstone of our non-fiction list, we publish an exciting range of travel, current affairs, biography, and popular science books as well. Our renewed focus on popular fiction is evident in our new titles by a host of fresh young talent from India and abroad. Jaico's recently established translations division translates selected English content into nine regional languages.

Jaico distributes its own titles. With its headquarters in Mumbai, Jaico has branches in Ahmedabad, Bangalore, Chennai, Delhi, Hyderabad, and Kolkata.

SINCE 1946